LIGHT BREAKING THROUGH

TRUSTING GOD'S TIMING

BILLIE CASH

AMBASSADOR
EMERALD INTERNATIONAL

GREENVILLE, SOUTH CAROLINA • BELFAST, NORTHERN IRELAND
www.emeraldhouse.com

Light Breaking Through:Trusting God's Timing

Scripture references are from the New International Version, unless otherwise noted.

Ambassador Emerald International
427 Wade Hampton Boulevard
Greenville, S.C. 29609 U.S.A.

and

Ambassador Productions Ltd.
Providence House
Ardenlee Street
Belfast BT6 8QJ, Northern Ireland

www.emeraldhouse.com

Cover design and page layout by A & E Media, Sam Laterza

ISBN 1 889893 97 8

DEDICATION

To

MY CHILDREN

Lieutenant Carey Hall Cash, USN (Chaplain Corps)
and
Kellye Cash Sheppard

God's Torchbearers

Proverbs 4:18

Acknowledgements

I want to thank my precious praying friends for praying me through once again.

All of life is a work of prayer.

I have an e-mail network of intercessors across this country who understand my ministry and faithfully respond to my "prayer alerts." You know how much I depend on you. The Calder Class in our home church has carried me in prayer. You are special. Laura Whybrew, Ann Slater, Denise Turner, my mother, Frances Hall and Judy DeMaio are praying women who believed in this project. Peggy Davis, Beth Kelly, Audrey McClung, Peggy McGaha and Hope Roberts pray me through all that I do, everywhere. I am grateful for each of you.

A special thanks for Judy Chatham's encouragement, my husband Roy's diligence in editing and Tomm Knutson's confidence in me. All of you are in my heart.

I want to thank my God for stretching me and causing me to dig deeply into His Word.

I rejoice in the path of the righteous.

I want a shining life.

I want my heart to grow ever brighter

I am closer now to Heaven and I look with longing and bright expectancy toward the city called Glory.

"Thank you, Lord, for trusting me to write and proclaim Your Path."

Billie Cash

FOREWORD

I know about stage light.

The actress prepares herself from the inside out. She studies the character's role in the play, how it fits into the dominant themes that the playwright has voiced. Perhaps there are interwoven threads of love, hate, ambition, revenge, success or failure to be dealt with in the story.

These are all elements of the human condition. In the rehearsal phase of the character development, there are lines to be memorized, blocking to be learned, staging to be directed and interaction to be developed among other characters. This is the process that must occur if the actress presents her part with ownership and believability to the audience. When this is completed, she then with great concentration and focus, makes up her face while she is making up her soul.

At last she is ready.
>
> The audience is waiting.
> The curtains are drawn.
> The stage light shines on her.

In that moment, the hard work and months of preparation come forth. The stage light can be flattering or brutal because it is artificial, but without it no one can see. The results lie in the skilled hands of the technical crew.

God's Light is also brought forth by great knowledge and skill. He is the Creator, the Master Director behind our drama. The one who knows each of us so intimately has seen us as we have played out the real themes of life on our own stage.

He knows our struggle,
>
> our aloneness,
> our brokenness,
> our darkness.

His Light is searching, knowing, penetrating. It takes us by surprise.

In triumph or trouble,

In delight or desperation,

In love or loss,

HE perfectly times moments of breakthrough, because of His Love.

Come along with me, dear reader, and let us experience LIGHT BREAKING THROUGH into our lives, intercepting us with truth, love, and insight at every turn, in every season. He is always urging us on, to continue, to grow, to believe, to love and finally to finish our race.

It is His Light.
It is Eternal,
Everlasting;
It is Enough.

We can trust His Light.

We can trust His Timing.

Billie Cash
Spring 2002
Cordova, TN

*ENDORSEMENTS**

David, the psalmist, observes: "In your light we see light" (36:9). This indeed is *Light Breaking Through*. It is only when God takes the initiative in our lives that we see light, which allows us to "walk in the light," that grows brighter each step of the way! This is what Billie Cash is teaching us in this delightful little book. Let us ever remember, however, that "light received brings light, but light refused brings night." So it is my prayer that God will bless the message of this book to readers everywhere.

Dr. Stephen F. Olford

Founder and Chairman of Olford Ministries International and Senior Lecturer at the Stephen Olford Center for Biblical Preaching Memphis, TN

* Additional endorsments on page 144

TABLE OF CONTENTS
*"The path of the righteous is like the first gleam of dawn, shining
ever brighter till the full light of day"*
Proverbs 4: 18

"The path of the righteous is like the first gleam of dawn, shining ever brighter till the full light of day."

Proverbs 4:18

CHAPTER ONE

COMING INTO THE LIGHT

Lead me from the unreal to the real!
Lead me from darkness to light!
Upanishad

Early morning light quietly steals into my bedroom through the open casement window.

A warm July day is awakening.

So am I.

The distant crowing of a rooster draws my mind into sleepy consciousness.

Startled by the shaking presence of Smokey, the brindled cat pouncing upon me, I am now awake!

He knows he lives here.

I am the intruder.

Strangely energized, I go straight for my walking shoes, shorts, and hat.

I am off on my first day in the New Forest.

Oh, the morning light in this English countryside!

Wonder is restored to the weary traveler.

The poet's heart is fed.

Wild donkeys greet one another and me as I breathe in the fresh air of this habitat. The sound of horses and riders on an early romp breaks the stillness.

Small bridges to cross and flowers spilling over the fences are my serendipities. A quiet church cemetery reminds me that many have walked this way and now rest here.

Birds share morning greetings.

Sheep roam and wander trying to find direction.

Much like we do.

A light jog carries me uphill into brighter light and then unexpected turns take me through the lower, shadowed, forested areas.

Contrasts reveal much on a walking path and on the path of life.

Nothing hustles here.

My numerous attempts with camera in hand can't adequately capture what I sense. One day while browsing in a second hand bookshop, I happened upon an exceptional pictorial book of rare photography entitled *An English Forest* by Richard Krause. He came upon the New Forest by chance in 1975 while visiting Southampton, the city where his grandfather was born. Perhaps he was searching for a link to the past. His fascination grew and he committed himself to a project involving five years of his life. Arising before dawn every day, his lens captured the "transient moments of the morning light" [1] found in the New Forest.

Scenes and seasons reveal life.

In his pictures, light breaks through tall pines and spreads to the great gnarled trunks exposed below.

Golden autumn dresses the earth with leaves of crimson, pumpkin and burnished brown.

The early mist of a winter's morn falls on a young fawn searching for food.

Summer grasses surround a mare and cradle a new foal as the miracle of life comes forth.

Pictures drawing me to a Creator.

Photographs revealing the Creator God watching over His creation – longing, waiting to be acknowledged.

Why?

Because of Love.

Whose?

His.

The photographer waits for the first light of dawn because it brings illumination…true focus is found in first light.

God waits for us to seek His light because it reveals the true condition of our hearts without Him, dead and darkened. Ephesians 5:8

We chase dreams, get a glimmer of His light but get lost in the pain of the past or the pursuit of the present.

He sends Jesus to the rescue.

Jesus said, "I am the light of the world."[2]

There is no darkness in Him

Just as the sun rises each day, the Son of God comes to show us our sin and need of Him.

Sin separates.

He came at a dark moment in history.

He died on a Cross, shedding His blood while we were "dead in our sins."[3]

He made a way where there seemed to be no way.

"I am the way, the truth and the life, no man comes unto the Father except by me."[4]

Jesus is Light.

He is the path to forgiveness.

Man stumbles in darkness without Jesus, wandering around much like the sheep encountered on my walk.

No leader.

No path.

Lost.

His sacrifice swallowed up sin then and now. Daily, we have access to hope and assurance because of Jesus.

Only Jesus.

He'll be the light.

But we try to find our own way. We run after dark dogmas and create our own theology of life. The center of the word "sin" has a large "I" in it.

We think our own light is enough.

But it isn't.

It leads to a temporary, driven, superficial life that gets bogged down in self.

Our light is so fleeting.

History shows us that many before us have come to this conclusion.

Dr. Stephen Olford's life as the son of a missionary to Africa is a poignant example. Young Stephen describes what he calls "…the trauma, trials and tears of the missionary life."[5] He finds the college years to be fraught with doubts about his faith. Disillusioned with the lack of godliness exhibited by Christians in the local church, he moves out into the world and steps back from his faith. So many interesting career directions, but he settles on mechanical engineering. Testing theories of carburetion by riding motorcycles and enjoying this sport becomes a passionate preoccupation. It's exciting to win trophies and notoriety. Stephen knows he is not living the life his parents would desire.

He's driven to create his own light.

Habitually he comes home late at night but always finds his mother on her knees praying for him. His father is serving in Angola at the time. One fateful evening, an accident occurs on the motorcycle. He suffers a severe concussion and pneumonia sets in.

No antibiotics,

No hope,

No telegram,

No father.

Rebellious against prayer and preachers, his darkness descends.

Two weeks to live.

Three months to get a letter to his father about his condition.

Three months to receive an answer.

Time is running out…or is it about to begin?

One afternoon, his mother slips into his room and drops a letter upon his bed. Immediately he recognizes the distinctive handwriting of his father. There is no possibility he could have known about Stephen's illness.

No way.

But there in that far away place, the Spirit of God Almighty has burdened this father to write these words – words to bring Stephen out of the dark.

"My son, this is of utmost importance.

Only one life, 'twill soon be past,

Only what's done for Christ will last."[6]

Suddenly God's light broke through to Stephen's soul.

He saw.

He knew his sin.

Falling to his knees, he faced the sovereignty of God, confessing his rebellion and his wayward life. A loving God is always pursuing us, wanting to save us from ourselves. He embraced the Light of Truth.

A mother's prayer,

A father's letter,

A changed life.

He promises to serve His God.

God promises to be his guide.

There are promises to the righteous, those who have opened their hearts and lives to a loving God. The righteous are those who are rightly related to Him. The righteous have tired of the darkness.

Tired of their sin.

The Light of God breaks through.

Because of Love.

He is forever seeking others hedged in hopeless boundaries. His powerful love reached long ago into the life of the great Helen Keller and freed her.

The literary style of this dynamic woman – sightless, deaf and unable to speak – is filled with references to the Bible throughout her writings. I visited her birthplace in Tuscumbia, Alabama years ago and was amazed to see a framed copy of the twenty-third Psalm hand-written by her. It was the most exquisite writing I've ever seen. I was told that she used a ruler. A sightless woman cared about her penmanship, cared about the writing of the Word of God! When the God-directed appointment came for her to interview with Dr. Alexander Graham Bell, immediately she felt his insight and acceptance. He began to discuss perspectives for her life. She then described that opportunity as the door through which she was to "...pass from darkness into light, from isolation to friendship, companionship, knowledge, love. I came up out of Egypt and stood before Sinai and a power divine touched my spirit and gave it sight. I heard a voice that said, 'Knowledge is love and light and vision'."[7] She had knowledge of God. Once again God's light broke in, bringing the light of hope and truth. Her life reflected true faith. She had a vision of God.

"The path of the righteous is like the first light of dawn, shining ever brightly until the full light of day." Proverbs 4:18

In order to embrace our God, we have to believe He knows us.

He knew Stephen and Helen.

In Psalm 139, the Psalmist tells us that when we were knitted in our mother's womb, He knew us. So, guess who has seniority in loving each one of us?

He does.

He delights in us.

He does not disappoint.

When we finally give up and choose Him, that's when we come into First Light.

"He has turned my darkness into light."[8]

No Jesus.

No Light.

Richard Krause searched the dawn for expressions of light.

Our God sent the perfect image of light to engage us.

He waits.

His Spirit prepares our hearts.

Then one day, we catch a gleam of His contagious love through someone's life that entices us, or a prayer that moves us,

or a scripture that's read to us,

or music that lifts us,

or a crisis that constrains us, and we are delivered from darkness into light.

The sinner uncovers the Light of Truth.

It is irresistible.

The path of the righteous begins.

It is the path to life.

When we come into His Light, we belong.[9]

His life becomes ours.

Forever.

Are you ready to explore His Light with me?

It is quite a journey!

Journal

Can you remember a time that you knew you were in darkness?

What did you do about it?

Is God drawing you to His Light today?

Will you receive or reject Him?

Do you believe He is Truth?

Prayer

Father:

Darkness is familiar. And this new path is unknown to me. I am tired of the old way. I am weary of my sin. I desire YOU, Jesus. Will You come into my life and light my way. I need eternal light, not a candle in the wind. Show me how to follow YOU. My sin has obliterated YOU for such a long time. Cleanse me. Forgive me. I do believe you gave your life for me long ago on a Cross – for my sin. Thank YOU. I choose YOU as my First Light, my Savior. Thank YOU for loving me to Truth. I desire to walk in YOUR Light all the days of my life. Now I know I am your child, I will never be the same. Thank YOU for hearing my prayer. I do believe.

Date:

CHAPTER TWO

THE LIGHT OF HIS FELLOWSHIP

I live and love in God's peculiar light.
Michelangelo

Books enthralled me.

Intriguing characters lived there.

They became my friends.

I internalized their experiences.

Moving around the country, as a child, did not provide many opportune moments for developing true friendship with others. I only attended thirty-three schools between ages five and seventeen! Dad's work as a road contractor put us on the road.

My books could travel with me and I traveled through them.

You know, when you are going to be leaving in a few weeks, people don't reach out, so I went inside – inside books.

It worked.

The world of literature opens up different ways of becoming.

"We want to escape the illusions of perspective on higher levels too. We want to see with other eyes, to imagine with other imaginations, to feel with other hearts as well as our own."[10]

I usually became the heroine of the books I read, if she triumphed, and I learned from her if she did not.

I grasped a lot about human relationships.

For example, I pretended I lived in Cornwall, England after I read the book *Rebecca*.

The rocky, northern English coastline, visible every day to drink in and absorb would be inspiring.

The difficult challenges she faced with people, trying to build relationships and be accepted. What a grand old house to ramble around in.

What a life she could have.

I understood Rebecca.

Raw material waiting for a chance to be developed into a real human being, that's who she was. Adversity framed her possibilities, but did not obliterate them. The incredible beauty of her surroundings bathed her wounds.

Beauty has that effect.

"Literary experience heals the wound, without undermining the privilege of individuality."[11] When I finished reading the book, I was still me, but I had a deeper capacity to understand life and was stronger in intent.

Books began to mirror my life.

God was drawing me even then.

I enjoyed poetry because the poet is always reaching for something just beyond his grasp.

Writing poetry gave me the expression I desired.

So did performing it.

I wrote a paper for my Oral Interpretation class in college on the poem *Renascence* by poet Edna St. Vincent Millet.

I also read it aloud for my class.

The poet cried out for rebirth to God, for another chance at life.

> "The heart can push the sea and land
> Farther away on either hand;
> The soul can split the sky in two
> And let the face of God shine through."[12]

Don't we all want that?

I lived in that poem for weeks. It had larger-than-life elements.

There was struggle, discontent and, finally, surrender.

This is our ongoing dilemma with God.

What we don't realize is that real fellowship with God is the key to friendship with man. He is the Creator God who knows each one of us and longs for us to know Him. Knowing He is present daily builds us, our character and our capacity to grow.

"God is present in the company of the righteous."[13]

He wants us to care about people.

That's His desire.

When we have a vital relationship with God, He causes us to want more, to search for more.

I saw the movie *Shadowlands* a few years ago. Since I knew it was the life of C. S. Lewis, I was eager to go. His multifarious faith, woven with scholarship, intellect and a quest for Truth, was captivating.

He experimented with so many "isms" and then one day he met Jesus.

Simple faith was born.

Lewis' journey interested me.

He did not have hordes of friends either.

In the film there was a conspicuous exchange between himself and a student. He had witnessed the student falling asleep in one of his lectures and had asked him to leave class. A few days later Lewis saw the young man in a bookstore.

He was stealing books.

Lewis then followed the young man home and confronted him.

Wonder why one sleeps through class ignoring books and then steals them?

The consummate teacher queried him, presenting a most relevant question.

"Why do you read?"

The young man's reply was insightful.

"I read to know I am not alone."

"That's me, Lord," I said.

He knew it was true.

He wanted to create within me a thirst for a deeper fellowship with him.

You see, if we belong to him, he is present – shouldn't we be?

That's relationship...and relationship becomes fellowship.

Years ago I read a tiny booklet published by Intervarsity Press entitled *Christ, My Heart's Home.* In the booklet the heart is described as rooms of the house. When we transfer the title to Christ, it becomes His house and he desires fellowship with us daily.

He is present and desires to be acknowledged in love. In the beginning of our journey, we have feelings and longings for Him but we're not sure what to do about them, so we get busy doing instead of being – action over relationship.

The hamster life begins.

Always on the wheel, sincerely pedaling – but going nowhere; that's us.

Women feel this way a lot.

Too much to do.

Too little time.

Too perfunctory in our God pursuit.

More duty than love.

The tiny booklet's illustration is not small. The woman of the house dashes toward the door one day and hazards a glance toward the den as she passes by. She notices that a fire is warming the room from the fireplace. Her Savior, with the light of the fire upon his face, is seated waiting for her, waiting for her to stop, take time, to meet with Him. She wants to, but she just doesn't have time.

Out the door she goes.

Her heart is pricked but only for a second.

Out the door she dashes!

How graphic this picture is. We want fellowship with God, but we have things to do, places to go, people to see.

So, we start living in the shadows.

There is light where there are shadows but it is not in focus.

It is not His Light.

He waits.

He knows we will need Him.

He desires fellowship with us. We get on the hamster's wheel.

We want action.

One morning when my young son Carey was two years old, I decided to clean out my kitchen cabinets. I was task oriented in those days and the job was way overdue. My mother had always told me that if a thought like that came over me, I should do it because it might not come back.

Order was very important to me.

My husband was overseas flying combat missions over North Viet Nam and I was trying to be all things. My daughter Kellye was seven years old at the time. On this day she was in school. My life was fairly predictable. I got up and fed the children and got Kellye off to school. I struggled the rest of the day with filling my time and caring for Carey and shrugging off depression. Cleaning the house was usually done at night so that I could wake up to order. That helped my frustration level and gave me more strength to take care of a rowdy, aggressive little toddler. The project appealed to me because it needed doing and I could control something.

I knew God was there. He was present but I was too busy.

I got everything ready.

Carey was playing in my bedroom and I became totally absorbed with what I was doing. It was really going to feel good, getting this done. Calling out to Carey every so often assured me that all was well.

So, I continued.

Suddenly I was aware of a strange silence in the house.

Fear gripped me.

I called for Carey and there was no answer; so I called again and still no response. I finally jumped up and went to look for him.

He was not in the bedroom!

I panicked and ran from room to room downstairs.

He was not there.

As I started upstairs, I saw the front door ajar. My heart sank and I began to pray, "Oh God, where is Carey? Please help me find him!" I went outside. Had he run down the road? Was he lost, confused or in danger? My neighbor, Mr. Koehl, was in his front yard. He saw me and sensed my unease. Together we began to call Carey's name!

Still no answer.

Frantic, I ran back into the house. My heart was throbbing and I was pleading to God with every breath. "God, I am trusting you." I shouted it and then I cried it out with tears streaming down my face!

This continued for I don't know how long. I knew I had to call the police.

Trying to calm down, I walked into the kitchen and saw my cabinet project spread out on the floor.

It was not so important any more.

I could not find my son!

Just before I determined to go to the telephone to call the police for help, a presence of assurance came over me, urging me to speak Carey's name out loud once more. I stopped and said "Son, if you are in this house, please answer mother because if you do not, I am going to call the police."

From underneath my heavy, gold and brown, woolen Italian bed-spread came a soft, impish little voice.

He said, "Boo."

I followed the voice and found him.

I began to sob.

Pulling him out from under the bed, I hugged him and we had a heart-to-heart discussion about what he had done.

He was playing hide and seek.

I was playing God.

I thought I was in charge that day.

I had my plans.

I did not have time to consult God.

I became too absorbed in what I was doing.

I forgot to check on my son.

I forgot my God was present.

He did not forget me.

He was present.

I discovered that day that I need His Light every morning.

He broke in that day.

I have never forgotten.

I had buried my life in books and run from people in my youth.

I buried my emotions in perfectionism and ran from the only One who would be my friend and companion as well as my Lord.

I had to be present for HIM.

There will always be projects to do and spaces to fill in our lives. The diversions we choose only satisfy for an instant. The heroines of my books had to learn how to live every day too.

Beds do go unmade.

Clothes need to be washed, folded and put up but they do reappear. The mundane in life must go on and we are a part of that process. We can neglect the ordinary or decide to synthesize it.

Both ways are dangerous.

God needs to be a part of our existence in a practical, intimate relationship. He will show us the right way to do what we must.

More of Jesus

More Light

More of me

More confusion.

I need His presence every day.

Don't you?

He is present to the righteous.

JOURNAL

Why do we make time for everything and everyone but God?

Have you been made aware that He wants to be a part of your plans?

Can you trust Him with the ordinary?

PRAYER

Father:

YOU are present with me. YOU are here. I present myself to YOU with thanksgiving and gratitude. I want to develop my relationship with YOU more and more. Forgive me for my selfish ways. I want YOU. I love YOU. Thank YOU for being patient with me. I need YOUR Light. Break through whenever I am out of focus. I praise YOU my Lovely Lord. YOU know my attempts to control. Shout to me when I hide! Make me disclose where I really am and compel me to trust YOU, my ever-present God.

CHAPTER THREE

THE LIGHT OF HIS APPRAISAL

Truths kindle light for truths
Lucretius

Tests troubled me in school.

I would study and prepare and sometimes actually get sick. In fact, I could have a fever during my exams and be healed when I had finished.

Why?

Because it was over.

Debilitating fear every time.

I wanted to achieve, to do well. That was an intrinsic part of my journey and there is much to learn and unlearn along the way. Being transient in school had conditioned me to have at least one thing that was always certain.

I would be prepared at exam time.

I would expend whatever was necessary to be readied.

I would finish what I started.

Always, I was appalled by those who ignored rules; people who went to a movie or stayed up all night, playing games during finals.

The living-on-the-edge crowd, who wing life.

I could not.

Today, I sense the same disparity found in busy, achieving lives. We dread that careful scrutiny from someone in authority, which is necessary for tangible success. I categorize leadership in two distinct styles based on my own experience.

There are evaluators and affirmers.

We think we know about evaluators.

They are tough.

The standard is uncompromisingly high.

Somebody is waiting for us to flub.

We do.

We have a mental picture conjuring up an assessment based solely on our ability to perform. You know, the divulging graphic of our good and bad days.

When we discover we are to be examined, we cringe.

Life, however, is perused by someone, every day.

What will I wear?

What if they don't like me?

What if I forget?

What if I fail?

"The Lord examines the righteous."[14]

Our God does examine us but he is the supreme Affirmer.

How can we know that?

His Love is unconditional.

He has the knowledge of our lives in His Hand – flaws and future.

He knows we will fail.

He never stops loving us, cheering us on toward victory. Thomas Edison said, "Many of life's failures are people who did not realize how close they were to success when they gave up."[15]

John Maxwell responds, "People think failure is final – it's not." [16]

It won't kill you.

Many times it is an intentional springboard that God uses in our lives to build faith and steadfastness, helping us to move forward the next time.

Godly character is chiseled in failure.

We don't abandon the program.

We keep moving on, knowing our God is working out the best plan for our lives.

He is never surprised.

We must not fear His appraisal.

He examines in love.

We are being trained to be His Life to a desperate world that views failure as the end of the rope.

It isn't.

It is the groundwork for true success.

As He unmasks our lives, the eyes of love search us and uncover the unusable spaces in our soul.

We all have them.

Sinners need His cleansing and empowering every day.

That's us.

We get broken and need to be redefined.

> Back to the potter.

> Back to the wheel.

> Back to the refiner's fire.

"We are not globs of clay that can be molded into whatever our parents or teachers want us to be."[17]

He has the design in mind for each life.

We are not here by chance.

Yes, we will be appraised daily in love by the One who made us.

He is the potter.

We are the clay.

We are all different pots and we have our own ideas.

Sometimes we want to be the creator.

We tell Him what we want to do and then try to put His name to it.

It doesn't work.

Years ago when I was much younger, I was scheduled to speak and sing at an event in California.

Excited and challenged, I was.

I remember saying out loud, "I know what I'll sing, I want to sing something very powerful, very moving." I prepared such a piece but I could not sing it.

The upper range of my voice was not there.

I had more than a vocal problem; mine was an "I" problem.

Something else had to be chosen.

I thought it was plan B but it was really plan A. What I sang was a simple rendition of Jesus Loves Me/Oh How He Loves You and Me.

That's what God wanted me to sing all along.

> He is the message.

> I am the vessel.

> He put me back on the wheel.

> I got the message.

What a joy it is to be cleaned up, filled and ready to be used by the Master.

"We are God's workmanship, created in Christ Jesus to do good works, which God prepared in advance for us to do."[18]

But we question God's ways.

At a Christian Writers Conference in 1981 in San Diego, I heard a frustrated young mother of two toddlers say to the seminar leader, "I know I can write, but I have these two children that keep me from it!" The wise teacher said to her, "My dear, they are your material.

God's light broke in on me that day.

God is always redefining us.

I have processed over and over those remarks. At that time, my daughter was in high school and my son was in middle school. I joined a writer's critique group and once a month we met to share our written work, to read it and have it critiqued. Sherwood Wirt, past editor of Decision Magazine, was the leader of our group. There was a truck driver, a lady with multiple sclerosis in a wheel chair, a man who had left the pastorate, a chatty, mid-life home-maker and me. Mr. Wirt said to me one day, "Keep writing Billie, you have something to say."

I did.

Timing,

Trust,

God's ways, not ours.

I wrote and kept prayer journals for years.

I wrote about what I know – my family and my relationship to God.

My first book, *Windows of Assurance*, was the result of this writing.

I praise Him for His ways.

I want to be used by Him in His way and time.

"Like clay in the hand of the potter, so are you in my hand." [19]

I am clay.

"Will the clay say to the potter, "What are you doing?" [20]

I have.

"Does not the potter have a right over the clay?" [21]

He does.

Service to God is a birthright, a sanction.

But He doesn't need you or me.

He allows us.

Babysitting in the church nursery is serving.

Chaperoning teens on a trip is serving.

Making a telephone call to a friend who is drifting away from God is serving.

Baking cookies for the nursing home is serving.

Praying for a soul in need is serving.

Extending yourself in any way to another BECAUSE Jesus impels you is service.

Practical, humble work.

It is not exalted.

Ordinary pots will do.

William Gurnall, a sixteenth century writer said, "God's timely intervention is a confirmation that you can believe his power is yours." [22]

God empowers us.

Gurnall also admonished us not to be envious of those who have many gifts. In fact, he suggests that we pity them and pray for them because God will have to do much to keep them clean and ready in order to be His instruments.

We must be sifted.

Wisdom comes from God.

He has perfect timing.

He knows when we are ready to serve.

He measures our progress.

We can pass inspection.

His power brings us into His Light.

Then we see clearly.

Pots are used in many ways.

Some pour out water on thirsty hearts.

Some provide food to those who are hungry.

Some deliver bread to those who do not know the taste of His love.

All are meant to carry nourishment to the weary, starved for a touch from Him.

Along the way, we get cracked and shattered and must be remade into something else.

He does the work in us.

He forms us.

We are made new many times in our lifetime.

Fragile becomes strong.

Flawed becomes beautiful with firing.

Finally we become.

We do His Work in the world.

Useful,

Pleasing,

Able,

Ready.

The furnace shapes us.

We shape the world.

JOURNAL

Why do we fear God's examination?

Does He love us?

Can we trust His timing?

Do we really want to serve Him?

PRAYER

Father:

YOU wait on us so patiently. YOU shape our lives and have a plan at the wheel.

We mess up and try to form our own vessel. We get broken. We fear failure and yet when YOU take our lives back into your loving hands, we are healed, redefined and made useful. Examine us. Keep us pure in motive and zealous in our pursuit of more of YOU. Show us how to serve YOU. Make us content where we are. Give us a sensitive heart and a keen eye today or we will miss YOU. Thanks for keeping track of us. We need YOUR appraising Light.

CHAPTER FOUR

THE LIGHT OF HIS SECURITY

A wave of light breaks into our darkness.
It is as though a voice were saying,
" You are accepted."
Paul Johannes Tillich

Secure.

Cherished.

Protected.

Beloved.

These words represent my God.

As a child I felt secure with my parents. Home was wherever we lived. It might be an apartment, a trailer or a real house.

We had many.

Learning to adapt was a way of life for my family.

Security comes from KNOWING.

What I did not realize then but what I now know is this; my God wanted me to comprehend security predominantly through His Word.

I needed to KNOW Him.

He is security.

As a nine year old, Jesus became my Savior.

When He got me, I got Him.

Eternal security began.

"We have this hope as an anchor for the soul, firm and secure."[23]

The journey ahead I did not know.

He did.

What could I expect?

He knew there would be constant change.

He knew I would be rejected.

He knew I needed stability.

He knew I needed to KNOW His Word.

> "Should the whole frame of nature round him break,
> He, unconcerned, would stand secure amidst a falling world."[24]

He would prepare me by His Word.

When He brings us into the light of His Truth and we embrace it, we have covenant together, as a child to a father.

We become family.

Ownership is entitlement.

We become His.

As children we trust.

His authority is a guarantee over us.

Then a wonderful phenomenon occurs, we become secure.

"He makes the righteous secure."[25]

We become stable through His Word.

How?

Every time we identify His promises to us from scripture, we discern more about ourselves.

What do we know about our God?

"Holy Father, protect them by the power of your name – the name you gave me so that they may be one as we are one."[26]

Our union with Jesus brings us into oneness with the Father.

Jesus prays for us.

That's security.

"For in Him we live and move and have our being."[27]

That's identity.

"Fix these words of mine in your hearts and minds...."[28]

That's comprehension.

He is steadfast and unmovable and we can be also.

"I have never seen the righteous forsaken."[29]

That's dependability.

"I write these things to you who believe in the name of the Son of God so that you may KNOW that you have eternal life."[30]

That's KNOWING.

Bonded together with eternity.

These are building blocks for the believer to fortify his life with strength in a frail world.

KNOWING the word of God provides a foundation upon which to build a life.

It is a love letter, an instruction manual filled with direction. It reveals the dark deeds of a crushed people who are forgiven and healed by the brightness of His love streaming into repentant lives.

Repentance cleanses us daily.

The revelation of truth.

A conscious turning away from our own darkness, sparked by His cleansing Light through our confession.

We can KNOW how to live if we live in the Word of God.

The more we live there, the more secure we become.

The little girl long ago did not understand all of this, but Sunday school teachers encouraged me to come to Bible Drill.

This was a teaching and training of how to know the books of the Bible and how to find scriptures quickly – within seconds.

I memorized whole passages of the Word of God. I wondered what in the world I would ever use this for!

GOD KNEW.

"Remember your Creator."[31]

He seemed to impress upon me – store up my Word my child, for when you have need of it, I will bring it forth.

I did and so did He.

Viet Nam, danger, loneliness, change, anger, pity, guilt, omission, desire, dreams.

Life to deal with every day.

He made a way for me to live because of the Word.

I lived in security.

"This word which sets us at once to work and obedience is the rock on which to build our house. Now the storm can rage over the house, but it cannot shatter that union with him, which his word has created."[32]

The crazier my circumstance, the more steadfast I became.

It worked in raising children and in marriage, in decisions of every kind.

I made mistakes but I understood why and recovered.

I could be restored.

My God forgives.

"Scrutamini scripturas (Let us look at the scriptures). These two words have undone the world."[33]

I was hungry for God's Word. Bible study became a vital part of my life. Loving the Word made my love for Him flourish and then I grew.

"He who dwells in the shelter of the Most High will rest in the shadow of the Almighty...He is my refuge and my fortress."[34]

Life does not always feel safe but that does not mean it is not.

Our faith is factual.

Our feelings are fickle.

Enduring faith born out of a living relationship in God can be lived out through the wondrous weight of God's Word.

We can possess an unwavering faith.

Her name is Becky. She is a precious woman of God and a dear friend. Several years ago a husband walked away from her, his children and from the church. She raised his little ones as her own from the time they were toddlers.

They lost their mother to cancer.

They lost their father to sin.

My friend lived with loss.

She mourned her soul mate.

She reconciled and loved an alcoholic father until he passed away.

She buried this cherished stepdaughter in her twenties to cancer.

She nursed her mother until her death.

She never wavered from her faith.

Becky became strong.

She never stopped loving God. She depended on His Word.

She studied it, savored it and wrote out her pain to Him.

Her life was crushed, but not destroyed.

Becky is secure in Christ Jesus.

A caring heart, a disarming smile, a warm hug, that's Becky!

The Word of God proves true.

EVERY TIME.

"Thy word is a lamp unto my feet and a light unto my path."[35]

Martin Luther learned that "The just shall live by faith."[36]

He was a man who searched out the scripture until the truth was settled within him. One day God's light broke in and he KNEW. He punctuated his teaching with illustrations like these. "As the meadow is to the cow, the house to the man, and the nest to the bird, the rock to the chamois, and the streams to the fish, so is the Holy Scripture to the believing soul."[37]

People choose how they will live. When they choose to live by the Word of God, they become confident, courageous champions to a world afraid.

How should we live?

Is it by the stock market?

Is it by achievement?

Is it in acquiring more?

I am certain change will come. Sometimes I will rejoice in it and sometimes I will be devastated.

It will do its work in me.

Left to my resources, I cannot recoup.

He can.

I can because of His life in me.

He "…is the same yesterday and today and forever."[38]

How do I KNOW?

I found it in the Word of God.

That's why the righteous are secure.

Is your security forever?

Mine is.

"Whoever trusts in the Lord is kept safe"[39]

JOURNAL

Where is my security?

Is the Word of God a significant part of my daily life?

How would my life change if I went to His Word daily?

Can I change at this season of my life?

PRAYER

Father:

YOU can change me. YOU want me to get to know YOU better and the knowledge of YOUR Word will help me. I have neglected this truth. I have tried many things. They were band-aids. I need surgery. I have wounds that need the healing authority of YOUR Word. I am hungry. I have lived off of the crumbs of others but YOU want to feed me from YOUR banquet table each day. Forgive me. I will become secure in YOU. Grow a love for YOUR Word in me. Keep me growing. Thank YOU for the Light of YOUR Word. I KNOW YOU will establish my way because YOU have plans for me. I rejoice in that security. It is forever.

CHAPTER FIVE

THE LIGHT OF HIS FAVOR

Mankind is a dream of a shadow.
When God-given brightness comes,
A radiant light rests on men.
John Henry Cardinal Newman

Have you ever experienced an entrancing moment so blessed that you knew the favor of God was resting upon you?

His lovely Presence embracing you with Light.

You know it is not yours.

It is His.

His alone.

I have.

A few years ago, I presented a musical concert in Plymouth, England on a Sunday evening at a church. The delightful and energetic senior pastor whose name was David suggested that we have a break for tea and biscuits in the middle of the concert and then I would resume singing. I had never experienced that before, but as a guest, I wanted to be sensitive to God's people. It is a joy to worship with the corporate body of Christ.

We have an innovative God and participating with Him is exciting. There is always a different way to do something. They staged the event with special lighting and provided an excellent sound system and skilled people to be in charge. Before the concert began, a group assembled for prayer. The pastors and lay leaders prayed earnestly for God's Mighty Hand to open the hearts of the audience to receive from Him.

They prayed for God's favor to be upon me.

"Look with favor upon a bold beginning."[40]

Virgil

I prayed He would.

I desire to be flexible wherever God sends me. This was a caring group of leaders. They loved reaching out. It was apparent.

I knew this was going to be an intimate time in the Lord.

It was.

The auditorium began to fill up quickly with many people from the surrounding area.

There were international college students from around the world and many others visiting from several local churches. I had prepared spiritually and musically for the concert.

I desired the favor of God.

The evening program included selections of music interwoven with my testimony, the story of my faith.

The lights dimmed almost to darkness. When I was introduced, a single light fell upon me. As I began to sing my faith to the audience, the sweet Presence of God came.

I sensed His Favor.

Never have I known such a flow of His Grace, a gentle anointing. It was as if I had lived my whole life in order to proclaim Him for that moment.

Effortless.

Empowered from above, I was.

I felt as though I had stepped out of my body and was watching someone else named "Billie" communicate His Love.

Every word was given to me.

It was a fountain.

His blessing and His presence were tangible. I wondered if the audience knew what I was experiencing.

Did they comprehend?

At the tea intermission, a Chinese college student came up to me and said, "Billie, what is it like to flow with liberty like you are doing tonight?"

I was taken aback.

He knew.

The audience had noticed.

I said, "This is an incredible gift tonight. I am a wife, mother and grandmother, a child of God. That's who I am."

He makes us aware of whom we are in Him.

"Now with God's help, I shall become myself," said Soren Kierkegaard.[41]

He knows when to bless us, when to restrain us.

This evening God took me to a new plateau of great favor.

I was overwhelmed.

>Humbled,

>Grateful.

We are set apart for a purpose – that the Christ we love and serve might be lifted up before a drowning world lost in darkness and thirsting for His Light.

He draws people to the Light.

He uses people.

He used me.

He'll use you.

I had never been so privileged.

I have never had a repeat.

We never do. Life is filled with moments. We manipulate some. Once in awhile we are readied for a touch of His Love that is recognizable.

Because it is His alone.

Many left that night with a fresh encounter from the Living God.

I was one of them.

There were tears and laughter,

>Confession and worship,

>Repentance and renewal.

We were enjoying His presence and it was magnificent.

God allows us to participate in moments of resplendent, unprecedented favor in order to reveal His Love for others. We are to be bearers of His life.

These are moments NOT of this world.

We cannot live there.

The air is too rich and we are too easily addicted to its aroma. We must live with our feet planted on the ground, looking up and reminiscing, reflective and ready.

FAVOR is also given to us in ordinary days.

It is perhaps most profound then.

God wants to lift up, encourage and comfort.

He uses ordinary people.

What happens is extraordinary.

Happenings occur every day.

A kind word fitly spoken to an impatient traveler in a security line at the airport,

A smile and a wave to an unruly youngster misbehaving in a restaurant,

A gracious hand extended to an elderly woman in the restroom,

A hug for the lady at the beauty shop, who works to make you beautiful,

A timely note to a friend who has suffered a miscarriage,

A basket of fruit to a neighbor who's had surgery,

A telephone call to a widow learning to walk with aloneness,

A visit to a nursing facility to give someone a touch of God's Love.

Every day people are drawn to the righteous, because He is in us. When we are aware, in tune with Him, on any given day, He spills over into the world around us.

His Light breaks through.

Do we make ourselves available for blessing?

"Surely, Oh Lord, you bless the righteous. You surround them with favor."[42]

We shall have blessing in order to become a blessing to others.

Therefore we should desire His favor.

When I look into the bright faces of our grandchildren, Brady, Cassidy, Tatum, Caleb, Justice, Phoebe, Nathanael and Ella Joy, I experience, with freshness and charm, the favor of my God.

They are stamped with His imprint.

He wants to bless them because He loves each one and has a destiny for each.

He bestows blessing freely upon the righteous.

It is our heritage.

When I hear Kellye sing or Carey preach, I sense the favor of God because He has called them.

Our God delights in giving His Love and Blessing.

Our soul bears His image. Obedience in the smallest act of love to anyone releases His favor.

He waits for us to be ready.

On December 23, 1987, I was boarding an Iberian airliner out of New York City with Kellye, Carey and John, a family friend. My husband Roy had command of an Amphibious Squadron, a task force of US Navy ships. The ships were to be in Palma Majorica for Christmas. This small island off the coast of Spain is a choice port for American ships. Carey was a senior in High School and Kellye had just relinquished the crown of her Miss America year. We had all prayed about this trip and saved our money. Roy felt it would cost us about $200 per day to rent a suite with three bedrooms in a hotel so we could all be together. We would be participating in a Christmas Eve service aboard the ship. Kellye was to sing. Arriving rested and ready seemed remote. Roy called me just before we left home and said "Pray. We might have an opportunity to rent a beach front apartment from a British couple for a very modest fee which would meet our needs amply."

That was to be the understatement.

Pray I did.

When we got to New York, a gentleman recognized Kellye as a former Miss America and asked her how many were in her party. She told him there were four. He then, without hesitation, escorted us down the walkway into the aircraft. Once inside, we were then directed up a spiral staircase to Deluxe Class. There were only about fourteen seats. The seats reclined; the food was gourmet cuisine.

We were speechless.

"Lord, is it possible that YOU arranged this just so we would arrive rested and ready for the service?"

He did.

Rested, fed, eager.

When the plane approached the gate, we spotted Roy and a Spanish friend, Alfonso. They were holding up a large banner. It read, "Merry Christmas, Billie, Kellye, Carey and John." He had some exceptionally good news. We had a three-bedroom apartment on the beach for the price of $40 per day! We shouted with delight at our good fortune and proceeded to the apartment to unpack and get ready for the service.

God had allowed our family to be together this holiday but there would be many young men there far away from home, lonely, missing theirs. I shall never forget what the Chaplain said as he stood before us dressed in camouflaged fatigues. He was talking about the shepherds who were in the fields tending their flocks on that night long ago. The Bethlehem Star appeared to them to direct their path to the Christ Child. "Those shepherds were out on maneuvers just like we are; away from home and look what happened. They were directed to the Savior. God knows where you are tonight and He cares about you and your loved ones. He will direct you and care for them."

How it touched my heart.

This man had God's Favor written upon his soul as he moved us to look for the Savior. He gave our faith a face.

It was Jesus.

"Forward! Thy orders are given in secret. May I always hear them – and obey.

Forward! Whatever distance I have covered, it does not give me the right to halt."[43] Dag Hammarskjold

We visited and ate refreshments with the men and rejoiced in the Christ of Christmas and in a God who is always arranging surprises for His children.

His plans require His Favor.

In May of 2002, Roy and I went to Colorado Springs, Colorado. Roy was scheduled to speak at the Air Force Academy to graduating seniors. He shared his career, leadership experiences, his principles for life, his belief in a strong family and a loving God. I had an appointment concerning my first book. We sensed God's leading in many ways on this adventure. On the weekend, we had looked at a vintage car with the prospect of buying it. To sort things out, we decided to go into a fast food place in the Denver area to get a bite of food. I approached the counter to place an order. A very pleasant African-American man spoke to me and took my order. He noticed my accent. "You are not from around here, are you?" I laughed and said, "No, I am from Tennessee." He then asked me what had brought me to Denver and I told him.

"I'm from Virginia; have you ever been there?" I then told him how many years we had lived in the Norfolk/Virginia Beach area. In fact, he began to reminisce about his grandmother who lived in an area called Seatack near Oceana Naval Air Station. I knew exactly where it was.

He was homesick.

Two Southerners had met. Friendly conversation was exchanged.

But there was more.

His story unfolded. He and his wife and four children had been brought to Colorado with the promise of managing a food franchise. "The promises made to me have not materialized."

I knew he was discouraged.

I said, "But God knows exactly where you are. He cares."

I then went to sit down with Roy. In a few minutes, the man came over to us with our food and this is what he said to us. "I am a believer and I was wondering if I could just touch both of you?"

We each extended a hand.

"Would you pray for me and my family? We are struggling." With that, we asked him his name.

"It's Carlos."

Carlos bowed his head. Roy and I asked God for blessing and encouragement upon this man and his family. He thanked us and we looked at each other with amazement.

God Almighty sent us to that restaurant and that young man because the family of God needed some reinforcement.

We are the brothers and sisters. They pray and God sends out the troops.

This time it was us.

The weather changed abruptly in the next twenty-four hours. Seventy degrees became twenty degrees. I needed a coat and one was provided for me without even asking. A mutual friend who lives there came to see me at the hotel and being aware of the drastic change, Eunice brought me a coat!

God is always ahead of us.

He's been preparing such appointments throughout eternity! Think of what we have missed because we were not looking at life through His lens.

When Bill Bright, founder of Campus Crusade for Christ, began to seek after God, he was drawn to a Bible class in Hollywood where Dr. Henrietta Mears was teaching young adults the Word of God. She was described as a "...dynamo, a seemingly tireless worker with a radiant personality. She was called 'Teacher.' It was as if everything she did and everything she said had a purpose. She spoke with authority, in flat, definite declarations bolstered by facts and her experiences. She had a global view of life and a fully integrated philosophy, mined by her study, refined by experience and molded and tooled for her life's purpose: introducing others to Jesus Christ and teaching them to do the same."[44]

A seeking heart had caused a loving God to arrange for Bill to be drawn to Himself through a Godly woman of Favor, God's Favor. Shortly thereafter, Bill Bright became a child of God and a deep desire to serve Him on the university campus followed. Campus Crusade for Christ exploded across America's colleges and around the world. Its impact has been profound. Thousands of young people have come to Christ and have become leaders.

Light to others!

Dr. Joon Gon Kim, Director of Korea's Campus Crusade For Christ said of Dr. Bright, "Sitting on a platform before millions, one doesn't get a sense of the mightiness and eloquence of the man, but of the mightiness of God."[45]

The Favor of God brings people into Light.

In the 1900s, in England, G. K. Chesterton described himself as a pagan at twelve and an agnostic at sixteen, yet his brilliant searching mind compelled him to look at Christianity and to investigate its claims. He became a spiritual father to C. S. Lewis. His writing was stirring and intellectually stimulating. Engaging as a debater and always full of mirth, one of his opponents, Cosmo Hamilton penned these words, "To hear Chesterton's howl of joy...to see him double up in an agony of laughter at my personal insults, to watch the effect of his sportsmanship on a shocked audience who were won to mirth by his intense peahen-like quarks of joy was a sight. I carried away from the room a respect and admiration for this tomboy among dictionaries, this philosophical Peter Pan...this gallant cherub, this profound student, this master, which has grown steadily ever since."[46] In pursuit of God, Chesterton found Him and with this knowledge and reality a great triumph of faith to the world was released! He declared, "I am the man who with utmost daring discovered what had been discovered before. I did try to find a heresy of my own; and when I had put the last touches to it, I discovered that it was orthodoxy."[47] He then took on any one in person or in print, who would presume to interpret the world apart from God.

Moments of Favor are a part of the path of the righteous. God's Light is always penetrating our hearts, showing us our sin, calling us to purity and then preparing us to be available.

I have experienced His Light breaking through from the examples found in biographies of men like G. K. Chesterton who was light to the scrutinizing world of academia.

I have seen the effects of God's Light Breaking through on the college campuses of America through Bill Bright's vision of bringing the Gospel to the universities.

I have sat in Bible classes where I have been riveted by God's Truth through a "Teacher" whose life and contagious faith have compelled me to develop my own.

We can know God's Favor on our journey.

Is there a "Carlos" in your future?

One such moment of His Light breaking through brings the applause of heaven!

Stage light ends with the performance.

God's Light is eternal.

JOURNAL

Do I really want the blessing of God?

As I become obedient, will He give more?

Is it Him that I really want to please?

PRAYER

Father:

What a wonderful promise YOU have given to me! I do want YOUR blessing. I realize now that YOUR Favor is given to me so that I might draw others to YOU. There have been times I have kept it for myself and even basked in it. Forgive me, Lord. All that I have has been given to me by YOU. It is YOURS. Help me to know that when YOU arrange an encounter for me, I will be given what I need. I will not fear. I will embrace YOU in every opportunity. Praise YOU. YOUR Light is eternal!

CHAPTER SIX

THE LIGHT OF HIS DELIVERANCE

Light breaks where no sun shines.
Dylan Thomas

Morning brings promise.

Why?

Because there is Light.

Night brings uncertainty.

Because it is dark.

God gave us both spectrums to live in and to ponder.

Have you ever stayed up all night with a sick child and felt if you could endure until morning, all would be well.

Morning came.

You survived.

In Judy Chatham's book, *A Whirlwind's Breath*, she reveals her journey through the care giving of two sons with potentially fatal illnesses.

In the weariness and struggle to overcome, perseverance and strength to believe God emerged.

She describes what morning is like for one who cares for an ill child. "Night. I know what it means to be a part of a night watch…I can see Nehemiah, of the Old Testament, as he secretly surveys the damage to the walls of Jerusalem…that weary vigilant one returns to the Valley Gate and says: 'You see the trouble we are in. We lie in ruins. Come let us rebuild.' And that is when the caretaker sees the first light of day, the morning light. The trouble remains, but there is a hope once more."[48]

Judy and her family did rebuild.

God intervened.

Healing and help were given to them.

And brighter faith.

God sees our real selves.

Anxiety at night.

Assurance in the morning.

Themes played out daily.

During the Navy years when my husband Roy was away at sea, I had time to contemplate many things. The day/night syndrome of my life certainly existed.

I dreaded the sunset.

I did laundry at night in the garage while my children slept.

As I worked, I would sing to my God.

He was my audience.

He always seemed close by when I would sing to Him.

I was not alone.

The words, "Help me make it through the night" became a prayer.

Roy's presence ensured Godly strength and protection.

When he was not there, I needed to believe that God was still with me.

HE was.

Singing to Him calmed my anxious heart and was a way of growing my dependence in HIM ALONE.

Music is a wonderful friend. Singing has always buoyed my spirit when I felt isolated or afraid.

"Forever singing as they shine,

The Hand that made us is divine."[49]

I wake up most mornings now with a song in my heart. Today it is the Brooklyn Tabernacle chorus, *All of My Help Cometh from the Lord.*

God's music has a pronounced influence upon our lives. It carries us through the dark places because it has the answer.

It brings His Light.

The tormented King Saul who was given to melancholy would call for his adversary David to come play music for him.

David did.

The Spirit of the living God would fall upon the troubled King as the mesmerizing music would become a balm to his soul and he would fall asleep forgetting that it was his rival who ministered to him.

There is a night season for us all. When it is dark in our souls, we need His Comfort, His Presence and sometimes HIS DELIVERANCE.

His music is one of the ways we overcome! It is the power of praise and it works!

"From the lips of children and infants you have ordained praise...

To silence the foe and the avenger."[50]

I find it fascinating that, frequently, when battles were fought in the Old Testament, the singers were sent in before the warriors.[51]

God's music parts the darkness. It prepares the way for victory.

It can become the horn of deliverance for the righteous.

"He surrounds us with songs of deliverance."[52]

> Disappointments
>
> Danger
>
> Disobedience
>
> Disillusion

We need the delivering Hand of our God.

> Illness
>
> Insult
>
> Insolence
>
> Infidelity

There is always some dark corner in our lives that is revealed when we least expect it and we cry out for deliverance.

"Get into right relations with God and all that God can do for you will be done. Become conscious of God and he can take care of you.... Everything, everything depends not upon making God conscious of you, but making yourself conscious of God."[53]

He does know us.

Sometimes we need to be delivered from ourselves.

The darkness is our own making.

We neglect God.

Self controls, making its own importance.

Sometimes succeeding.

A loving God takes the night watch and knows when to break through.

Drawing us back to Him, we can finally see where we left Him.

Self diverts, dictating a new strategy.

We fly headlong into situations, fooling ourselves into thinking this must be God's Will. The offer is so special, so out of the ordinary.

If we tack His name onto it as in a postscript, surely it will be what He wants for us.

Self repositions God, managing His influence.

One such temptation came my way when we were living in Burke, Virginia.

Roy was stationed at the Pentagon in Washington, DC. Carey was a five-year old in kindergarten and Kellye was in middle school. A phone call came from a Bible teacher who had been having a Bible study for staffers at The White House. She was being transferred and was trying to find someone who would be able to continue the Bible class. I was approached to do it. The lady was emphatic that I was "the one." It was as if God had told her so.

She had never met me!

Logistically, I would have to drive from Burke, Virginia to 1600 Pennsylvania Avenue and be in place to start by 8:00 AM once a week. That alone would be an hour's drive if there were no unusual traffic or weather problems. The study and preparation would be extensive. I was already committed to the chairmanship of a Christians Women's Club that year and my children were in two different schools. If you have lived in Northern Virginia, it would be apparent that any involvement like this would require major adjustment. My son and daughter would have to be left with someone and gotten off to school for my husband left before they did!

BUT –

Dark whispers hovered over me.

What an honor to be asked.

They want YOU.

Great pride welled up.

until –

I asked God to show me.

The answer was no.

One has to get over the honor and get to the responsibility.

Is this your will, Lord?

If it is your will, give me peace and provide all that I will need.

I got delivered FROM myself that day and only God knows what else!

Self lost.

It was an insightful lesson I have never forgotten.

The Sovereign God reigns over the righteous.

"God...gives songs in the night."[54]

"O souls in darkness groping,
    And looking for the light,
Oh look to Jesus only. With Him is love and might.
    Believe that He is able to lead you into light."[55]

We are also delivered THROUGH circumstance by His Hand.

It was August of 1998 and we had just moved into our home in Cordova, Tennessee. There were three months of renovation to be done and we were adding on a sunroom. Boxes, disorder and stuff were everywhere.

Exhaustion was building in me.

Why, I could set up a house in ten days – max. Hey, I'm a pro at moving. It's all I've ever done.

I was scheduled for my annual mammogram and shortly thereafter learned that I must have a breast biopsy.

Shaken I was.

This was not an obvious lump. Only mammography could have revealed it. Fatigued from the move, I now had another mountain to add to my overload! Refusing to cave in to stark terror, I remember praying, "Lord, I need a plan in order to prepare for this surgery. Show me your way."

He did.

The plan was to read and meditate on His Word and sing to Him every day. Once again God used praise to penetrate my soul.

His music has the answer.

I would sing with music tapes, and give my praise back to Him as an offering. As long as I was singing God's praise and reading his Word, I trusted, but when I was not, I had fear.

Our minds are the battlefield.

Fatigue and fear tend to crush faith and suffocate trust.

The struggle to trust God exclusively is a part of every Christian journey.

The night before surgery, Roy stayed awake and prayed for me all night. He knew how tired I was. He prayed for me to sleep.

I did.

Morning came.

Scripture hung on the wall over the receptionist's desk at the hospital.

"Trust in the Lord with all your heart and lean not on your own understanding.

In all your ways acknowledge Him and He will direct your paths."[56]

I needed to trust.

The darkness began to lift.

A delightful nurse came and rolled me in a wheel chair from Methodist Hospital over to U T Bowld Hospital where my admitting doctor's office was. The two hospitals are connected by a long cross walk. She initiated the conversation by saying, "Isn't God good?" My spirit soared.

His Light was breaking through!

She hummed *Amazing Grace* as we entered the connecting corridor and I began rejoicing in His Presence. I almost catapulted out of the wheel chair!

The doctor who was to prepare me for surgery was waiting to discuss the best angle for the needle biopsy. The area in question was hidden near the wall of the chest so careful and exact precision was needed.

I replied, "Doctor, don't worry – there is an army praying for us." His face brightened and he said, "Oh, you must be a Christian, Mrs. Cash; so am I."

Hallelujah, my God was giving me a faith lift at every turn.

Light continued to break through.

Then I was wheeled into surgery. There was much difficulty in finding a vein for the IV. The surgeon said, "Keep praying, Mrs. Cash, I must have a vein."

She knew I was.

Words of scripture came to mind, and I said, "They overcome by the Blood of the Lamb and the word of testimony." Then, "Lord, she needs a vein, Lord."

"I've got it," she replied."

Those were the last words I remember.

I came home that afternoon from the hospital. Several days of recuperation went by and I left for Birmingham, Alabama to speak. We were still awaiting the final test results. When Roy called me, I was singing *He's Been Faithful*. He said, "Honey, all is well."

Indeed we must stand on what we know and trust God for what we don't. A watching world must see and hear a specific act of deliverance from a caring God.

He brings us THROUGH because the righteous are HIS ministering people.

The triumph is His alone!

"You were once darkness, now you are light (for the fruit of the light consists in all goodness, righteous and truth)...but everything exposed by the light becomes visible for it is light that makes everything visible...."[57]

In June 2001, my book, *Windows of Assurance*, was scheduled to arrive stateside in Greenville, South Carolina on a Wednesday. Sam, the graphic artist, was working on it while on the island of Saipan, one of his stops on a far eastern trip to China. The timing was critical if it were to be ready to go out to the printers on the following Friday. This was necessary if it were to be released at the International Christian Booksellers Convention in Atlanta in July. I had a network of committed believers who had prayed through the stages of this book.

I was trusting God's timing.

The book arrived in South Carolina, but the e-mail to me from the publisher said, "We don't have a clean print out."

I was devastated.

I was about to enter "a whirlwind of grace and tempest."[58]

That morning I was shuffling around in my bathrobe as one wandering aimlessly, stunned at the circumstance but determined to BELIEVE! We had prayed through some delays before but now we were down to the wire. There seemed to be no way humanly possible this book could be "fixed" in one day and be ready to be shipped on Friday.

I was weak in spirit and spent in body.

That morning I said, "Lord, show me some scripture I can pray in faith. I want to pray your Word. By faith, I still believe you can make it happen." I was directed to II Chronicles 20 to the prayer of Jehosaphat. He was overwhelmed at the vast army coming against him. In verse 12, we read, "For we have no power to face this vast army…we do not know what to do but our eyes are upon you." Beside that scripture in my Bible, I wrote, Book 2001 – desperate! That's how I felt!

"Lord, there's probably only a few folks who really care about meeting this deadline in Atlanta – You, me, Roy and Judy."

I read on in the chapter that after Jehosaphat inquired of the Lord, he was told in verses 15-17, "Do not be afraid or discouraged because of this vast army, for the battle is not yours, but God's. You will not have to fight this battle. Take up your positions; stand firm and see the deliverance the Lord will give to you. Go out and face them tomorrow and the Lord will be with you." Then he bowed with his face to the ground and worshipped the Lord. He called the people together and told them to have faith in God and they would be successful. The last thing he did was to appoint men to sing praises to God and they went out ahead of the army.

Ambushes were set against the enemy.

The awesome power of God's music disarmed the enemy for it parted the darkness and His Light broke through giving victory that day!

What a pattern to pray!

I stood in my sunroom that morning and I prayed these same words back to God.

I prayed them out loud.

"Lord, I take my position and stand firm. My position is this. I am your child. My sins were covered by the Blood of The Lamb. I belong to you. I believe You will deliver this book because it is Yours. I trust in You.

YOU ALONE."

Then I got down on my face and worshipped my God and when I got up,

I realized that I had not sung in about three days.

Fanny Crosby, blind her whole life wrote, *Blessed Assurance* in her late eighties. God gives us music to "inspire and nurture our experience in Christ."[59]

She had assurance and wrote about it.

I had it too and needed to sing it!

There was a song I was learning, an old song but new to me. I put the music tape on and I began to sing *The Anchor Holds*. My ship was battered and my sails were torn. I had been on my knees and then I got on my face. I had faced the raging seas and the anchor does hold in spite of the storm. I marched around my kitchen as I sang and the more I sang the more I believed.

At 11:30 am, an e-mail came in from my publisher. "I have some good news, Billie. We have a clean print out."

I dissolved.

The anchor held.

Light Broke through.

God gives songs of deliverance to the righteous!

Journal

What do you need deliverance FROM?

What do you need deliverance THROUGH?

Will God send deliverance BECAUSE you will use it for His Glory?

Prayer

Father:

YOU are my Deliverer and sustainer of life. Praise YOU that the impossible is what YOU are all about. Today I take my stand and believe. I fall on my face and worship YOU. I hold on to the anchor. I know the Light will be breaking through every time because YOU are my refuge. What an exciting way to live.

CHAPTER SEVEN
A SHINING PASSION

*Someday, perhaps the inner light will shine forth from us
then we shall need no other light.*

Johann Wolfgang Von Goethe

There is a beguiling scene in the play, *The Rainmaker.*

Lizzie, a spinster in her late thirties, the only daughter of a widowed rancher, is wooed and charmed by a flamboyant nomad. He claims he can deliver rain. It's desperately needed. A severe drought is underway.

He is hope.

A charismatic character, he uses words to flatter and flutter her heart, telling her she needs a new name, a more fitting one, an exciting one like his – Starbuck!

The name Lizzie is just too plain.

Just think of it.

What an adventure could be hers if she would just take off with him in search of whatever it is they don't have.

This is insanity.

Leave the familiar.

Leave for the dreams of last chances.

Ever thought about doing just that?

He tries to pull it off.

In an intimate scene out in the tack room in the barn, Starbuck suggests that she let down her hair.

This is no small task.

Her long, disheveled, scraggly, brown hair was always rolled up into a tight fisted bun at the nape of her neck. A kiss is given.

One might assume that it was the first ever and could be the last in her life.

You see, Lizzie was plain.

Timing is important.

For one shining moment, she felt loved, accepted, fulfilled and beautiful!

Of course the starry, moonlit night helped.

It was dark.

In the morning, however, the spell is broken and Mr. Prognosticator splits.

There is no rain.

Life continues as before.

Lizzie is still plain.

In a shining moment, I played this character and received lovely applause for a convincing performance as well as an award at White Station High School for "Best Actress."

They liked me.

I needed affirmation.

To move people, to touch their hearts, to cause them to laugh or weep, to bring them to another level – that is the role of the actress.

My passion was unveiled.

Trophies, medals, and awards are the stuff of theatrical passion.

Passions take us places we've never been and once we get there we don't want to leave. They fill an ache or a void.

We CAN be good at something, right?

All those empty spaces in my childhood needed expression.

Fear, few friends, forever moving – that was me.

A shining moment of adulation does temporarily erase a lifetime of piercing arrows.

The theatre birthed belonging.

It worked.

I discovered talent was the door to acceptance.

Years later when I read the book *Sacred Romance,* I knew at once that my romance with the stage was an attempt to bury rejection. By performing well, I gained the respect and favor of those very people who had ridiculed and wounded me.

Those were my arrows.

It seemed like a fair trade-off at the time, but the life of my heart was still seeking after more – some missing element. Success on the stage certainly isn't permanent. I was always pressured to recreate. Inside was a deep longing that would not go away. There had to be a bigger picture that I was to be a part of and guess what?

There was.

God was drawing me to Himself. The Lover of my soul was wooing me. John Eldredge describes this yearning of the heart as a "longing for transcendence, the desire to be a part of something larger than ourselves, to be a part of something out of the ordinary that is good."[60]

That was it!

His book was a startling disclosure of truth for my hungry, thirsty, seeking heart.

It was a shining moment of redeeming my whole life experience. I saw it, as in a flash, from God's perspective! My story was to be a unique part of His story and this is true for each of us!

He had wooed me as a child to His Love.

He wooed me from the theatre.

He wooed me into His Word.

He wooed me by His Presence.

He wooed me back to Him.

Christ Himself was tracking me and loving me into a complete union of communion with HIM!

Years of waiting for my surrender,

The everlasting "repairer of the Breach" repaired me.[61]

He was victor.

"As a deer pants for streams of water, so my soul pants for you, O God.

My soul thirsts for God, for the living God.

Where can I go and meet with God?"[62]

My passion turned from its own pursuit to HIS.

I cannot remember exactly when it happened, the moment. It was as if my search for significance was over because Significance had found me. What is even more encompassing is this; all other loves and interests became absorbed into this Consuming Love. For it was this Love that motivated me to be, to serve, to integrate my life with others because His Heart is for people.

I didn't love less.

I loved more.

He brings balance to passion because He is the unifying Force.

He determines much or little, forward or backwards, empty or full.

He establishes the standard.

Our passion for Him is sustained through obedience.

Suddenly, purpose is raised up in our lives. Filled up with His Love, we begin to shine! The light that we reflect is His Light and we are not even aware of it.

We cannot maneuver or negotiate it. It is the product of devotion not activity.

The world needs to experience an up close and personal God who knows each one by name and is longing for a love relationship. If we choose to grow in that love relationship to Him, others will see His Love and believe. Our triumphs and defeats are then lived out in faith not theology.

They are visible.

Henri Nowen insisted his pursuit of God could be looked at, probed and questioned. He challenged others to consider a search, a personal seeking after God and "…all of his reading passed through the filter of his own experience."[63]

I like that.

"The strength of his writing is this ability to combine knowledge with personal experience."[64]

When our lives are opened to God, they can be opened before man and guess what? Whether we like it or not they will be. Everything must be looked at through the windows of our own understanding.

What does God want from us?

What do we want from Him?

Do we want to please Him?

Do we thirst after Him?

In the fourth century, Augustine said, "Who shall give me the gift of resting in you?"[65]

He knew what passion turned loose outside of God was like.

He "...was in love with loving."[66]

It was his life style until he met the Savior and his passion turned. The Savior's passion is about redeeming lives.

Augustine was redeemed.

A restless heart is in danger.

A heart resting in Him is at rest.

It is a struggle to rest, is it not? There are so many pulls on us today.

Identity, love, relationships, self worth, success, failure – all reality checks.

But what about dreams and hopes for the future?

Does God participate in them?

Do I care about a world that needs redeeming?

What part does my passion play in the big picture?

In fact, does He have dreams for you and me that we do not know about?

I believe He does.

I am stretched by looking back at some of the great heroines of the faith and one such woman was Madame Jeanne Marie Bouviere de la Mothe Guyon.

That was her complete given name! Can you imagine a name like that?

Writers refer to her as Madame Guyon. She lived during the seventeenth century during the reign of Louis XIV. It was a time of great affluence and deep moral decadence. Women had spiritual directors who advised them on all matters. Early in her life, she began a restless seeking after God. Married as a child bride, to an older man, she was thrust into a loveless marriage with a difficult mother-in-law. Every move she made was perused by this suspicious woman. Once she was told to come and sit in a room all day so that it could be noted how she behaved. If she prayed too much it would be a cause for alarm. So Jeanne Guyon, as a naïve young wife, had no liberty or love in her marriage.

A search for identity led to a search for God.

Unhappy and unable to please her husband and mother-in-law, she would seek counsel from her spiritual director.

Her heart began to cry out for God.

A wise monk told her that she must seek after God through her heart. She knew he was right. It was the turning completely to her Lord in a supernatural instance that made her know.

"O, my Lord, you were in my heart. And you asked from me only a simple turning inward to make me feel your presence. O Infinite Goodness, you were so near, and I went running here and there to look for you, and I did not find you. My life was miserable and my happiness was within me. I was in poverty in the midst of riches, and I was dying of hunger near a table spread and a continual feast. O, Beauty Ancient and new, why have I known you so late? Alas! I was seeking you where you were not, and I did not seek you where you were. It was for want of understanding those words of your Gospel when you say, 'the kingdom of God is not here or there, but the kingdom of God is within you.'"[67] We live by faith from our heart and only God changes the heart.

> Passion turned.
>
> Found by Him,
>
> Loved by Him,
>
> Sustained by Him.

This is what she faced in the years to come.

Smallpox robbed her of her beauty. She lost children and her husband.

Alone.

With each setback, loss, her passion for Jesus grew brighter.

People came to her for counsel because her life was enveloped with the lovely fragrance of one who knows God. She broke open her alabaster box and gave what she had.

Always she wanted to know more.

Some received and some were repelled.

Some discredited her.

She began to write.

Some received and some were repelled.

There was a cost.

Persecution followed.

Prison – and then eternal reward.

WHAT SHINING PASSION for JESUS that would not die!

We are still reading about her life, and she is still gathering fruit for His Kingdom.

For years, I busied myself with many passions.

The theatre was a monopolizing hobby, but developed confidence in me.

Collecting was an obsession, for antiques reflected a heritage. I wanted roots.

Wardrobing was a crazed interest because fashion is always changing, dictating identity and breeding discontent.

I needed an identity sculpted in Christ Jesus.

Decorating was a frenzied pursuit. It was never the same, too large, too small, too expensive, always a calculation to be reckoned. I wanted to create beauty around me.

When my pursuit of many became the passion of ONE, my heart found its mission.

To bring honor and glory to my King and to serve Him all of my days!

What He promises is true and eternal.

Is the life of women today far removed from Jeanne Guyon's?

Women are trapped in loveless marriages.

They hunt for something new to taste, wear, build or try out.

Loss comes.

Children leave.

Relatives criticize.

Defeat is a breath away.

The search for an everlasting love is everlasting.

Until the love of Jesus knocks at the heart's door.

The great Love of our lives is finally discovered.

His passion for us becomes ours and it is shining!

"The Road ever on and on
Down from the door where it began,

Now far ahead the Road has gone,
And I must follow, if I can,
Pursuing it with eager feet,
Until it joins some larger way."[68]
 J. R. R. Tolkien

Passion must have a home.

Journal

What is the great passion of your life?

Have you found your mission?

Are you serving another master?

Prayer

Father:

YOU are a consuming fire and I want to serve YOU. Forgive me as I have sidetracked my life so many times with other pursuits. I want to live and breathe YOUR dreams. I lay mine down. I believe YOU have work for me to do that no one else can do quite like me. I want YOUR joy and contagious love to spill out of my life daily. I want to intercept the lost, struggling and bound and show them the way home. It is through the Cross. YOU keep YOUR promises and I want to keep mine. Praise YOU for coming after me, passionate Lover of my soul.

CHAPTER EIGHT

A SHINING PRAYER

Hail, Holy Light...
John Milton

It was the summer of 1963 and I was a new bride of a few weeks.
My husband Roy was in Navy flight training at Pensacola, Florida.
He was scheduled to leave for survival training over the weekend.

I was to be by myself for the first time.

Our small apartment backed up to Pensacola Bay. When storms
came through, we witnessed the effect.

A weather alert forecasting heavy winds, high tides and rough seas
for the next forty-eight hours was announced.

It concerned me.

In fact, a hurricane would be skirting the coastline and we would be
experiencing the tail! So not only was I going to be alone, but a real
storm was coming.

As a child, I always needed a night-light and this night I kept all my
lights on. By mid-day, whipping winds began to howl. The waves
were slashing the beach behind our "honeymoon" cottage. Fortify-
ing myself for the night with *Gone With the Wind*, I thought I was
prepared. I had never read the novel in its entirety. Now seemed to
be just the right time.

It was.

The darker the night grew and the louder the storm, the more I
clutched my book and kept reading, hoping I would be safe and Roy
would be too, wherever he was.

I shot up a prayer or two like a telegram, nothing detailed or profound.

I did not bother to read the Bible.

I was into the struggles of Scarlett and her feeble attempts to get her
own way.

It was a noisy, edgy night and I read through it, finishing the novel
by daybreak. Exhausted, I fell into a fitful sleep and slept until
lunch.

I did not know that prayer training was on God's agenda for me.

As a Navy wife, I would have many storms to deal with.

Some were real, some imaginary.

I needed to learn to pray. This storm came and left. Roy returned home hungry but unscathed.

I continued to shoot up prayers every so often when we had an argument or when I wanted something, but most people do that. It was not until my children came along that I felt the overwhelming need to learn to pray.

"Teach me how to pray, Lord. I want to be a woman of prayer."

1972 was the year I started learning. Viet Nam was raging and Roy was overseas. I needed to enroll in the school where no one who loves God ever graduates.

I needed a praying life.

I needed a growing faith.

Great is thy faithfulness, Oh God my Father!

"Because of the Lord's great love we are not consumed, for his compassions never fail. They are new every morning...the Lord is my portion, therefore I will wait for him."[69]

Will I learn to wait upon the Lord?

Is there more to prayer than just asking?

Is it a way of life?

Questions that needed answers and a life that needed to know how to live.

Prayer would be the key.

His key for me.

Praying is keeping vigil. I needed to become a watchman.

"I have posted watchmen on your walls, O Jerusalem,

they will never be silent."[70]

A watchman is vigilant.

"Arise, cry out in the night, as the watches of the night began, pour out your heart like water in the presence of the Lord. Lift up your hands to him for the lives of your children."[71]

Need was the driving force for me. God's Word was my prayer many times as my own words were inept when my heart was crying out. Gradually I saw a larger truth concerning prayer, which until now was foreign to me. My reasons for wanting a praying life were completely selfish. I wanted to be effective in order to pray for my own. My God, however, wanted me to pray for others. Prayer is the great work of the church.

We are the church.

Since every believer is a stone in His building, we each must contribute our part. Intercession is the center of God's heart and that's where we each need to live.

"The Lord looked...

He saw there was no one,

He was appalled that there was no one to intervene."[72]

NO ONE TO INTERVENE

We can't manufacture prayer.

It is a circle of love, not duty. Our Father could grant any wish, cure any illness or answer any request.

He does not have to use us. He allows us to participate. Why He chooses us, pitiful, puny people to pray, I do not know, but He does.

I do know this – I am one of them.

The more I give myself to prayer, the more I desire to pray. The more I am in prayer, the more I love Him and the more I love Him, the more I love the one I am praying for.

"But because Jesus lives forever, he has a permanent priesthood. Therefore he is able to save completely those who come to God through him, because he always lives to intercede for them."[73]

Amazing to comprehend.

A permanent high priest who lives to intercede for others.

For you and me.

Jesus is the door to intercession and we open that door for others.

To be effective pray-ers and to do the bidding of our Father,

We must know Him through Jesus.

We must be clean vessels with our sin confessed.[74]

We must be filled with His spirit and we can ask for that.[75]

We must be dressed in the full armor of God.[76]

Then we are ready.

Ready to intercede.

"If the key is prayer, the door is Jesus Christ."[77]

Many of us would rather do for God than be in His Presence.

At one time, Henri Nowen was struggling with many issues in his life and decided to visit with Mother Teresa. After trying to explain all the complications of his life to her, she said, "Well, when you spend one hour a day adoring your Lord and never do anything which you know is wrong...you will be fine." He said, "Her few words became engraved on my heart and mind...I had not expected these words but their directness and simplicity cut through to the center of my being. I knew she had spoken the truth and that I had the rest of my life to live it."[78]

Are we willing to be the body of Christ in this world through a praying heart?

Amy Carmichael was.

What a shining, praying life she had.

No other woman's biography that I've read so represents a life

Called out,

Completely devoted,

Committed to Christ,

Consecrated for a cause close to God's heart – saving children.

The story of the Dohnavur Fellowship in South India is the ministry of her life. She arrived in 1895 and remained there without furlough until she entered heaven in 1951.

What a story of courage, faith, perseverance, love, vision and sacrifice all carried by prevailing prayer. My faith has been enlarged forever by this woman's story. I wept and rejoiced as I saw the mighty

Hand of God reaching out to rescue and restore Indian children sold and abused in temple worship. Her delicately restrained use of graphic language leading the reader to know the hideous truth had to be revealed to her through prayer.

Yet one knew.

"The child told us things that darkened the sunlight. It was impossible to forget those things. Wherever we went after that day we were constrained to gather facts about what appeared to be a great secret traffic in the souls and bodies of young children, and we searched for some way to save them and could find no way."[79]

These were words written in the beginning when the call of the work was impressed upon her soul. It seemed hopeless and desperate and yet she embraced the task with bedrock belief in the only ONE who could do it. Amy prayed through and God opened heaven for her. As the work progressed, the pattern given was to seek the Lord in prayer and wait upon Him. Every worker who came and joined the staff was called through prayer. Their plans were to pray, wait for monies to come, pray and build as needed.

They prayed for provisions.

Provisions were provided.

The little prayer bell rang at noon and all stopped for prayer. There were days of prayer when decisions were to be made concerning every detail. Little girls were the first ones retrieved from this horror and in time so were the little boys. Step by step with careful planning the work unfolded. Nurseries abounded everywhere but so did graves as many fought illness and did not make it. They were given names like Pearleyes, Jewel, Cuckoo and Moonflower.

I can picture the faces of these beautiful children gathered up, held and loved. Then they were given Jesus and they grew in favor with God and man and became men and women of prayer and power.

Setbacks evolved, court battles, disease, mouths to feed and bodies to clothe but always she had the vision of a Loving Christ who would provide and HE did. The astounding faith of one who so believed when there was not a glimmer of visibility on the horizon challenged those with hollow faith.

They kept journals about the work.

More vision,

More buildings – a house for prayer and a hospital were added. This little consecrated band of people met with God and experienced Him daily.

Miracles happened.

Children were taught order and faith.

Godly character prospered.

How did this work survive the onslaught of wickedness? After all, they were invading enemy territory with God's Light.

IT CAME THROUGH PRAYER.

When the hard places arose – and they did – a note was received, some monies arrived, a word from the Lord through scripture, a song. They prayed until unity and singleness of purpose were found amongst them. It was a family unifying itself under an Omnipotent God, dependent on Him alone. He gave them great beauty to refresh their lives. There were rich sunsets and brilliant sunrises, exotic flowers, fragrant forests, billowing seas, lush green valleys, rolling mountains, blowing winds, pelting rain, and chirping bird song to remind them of His creation. When loneliness laughed at them, His lingering smile was there.

He is enough.

They had a vibrant living relationship with a personal God who knew each one by name. As they grew in loving Him, their praying lives began to shine with expectancy and hope.

India was never the same.

Neither were they.

Neither are we.

"This method of divine leading – by the hour and by the moment leaves the soul free and unencumbered, and ready for the slightest breath of God."[80]

Madame Guyon

What do we learn from this beloved missionary, Amy Carmichael?

Prayer is the way God changes the world. We who pray are changed the most.

Life gets broken and so do we.

Darkness comes every day to some corner and we can't physically go to every corner – BUT God can call us and we can pray with perspective and a fervent heart.

We can pray for those dark corners.

Sometimes they are around the corner from us.

There was a February in Burke, Virginia when our electric bill was over $300. It had been a cold and snowy month. We were staggered at that amount.

We did not have it. There was, however, an anticipated check from another source of income that we received every spring. It wasn't due for about six weeks.

I prayed for provision.

It came early.

The bill was paid.

Our faith grew.

Light in a dark corner.

There was a hot August in Newport, Rhode Island that I remember. Roy was there for The Naval War College course of graduate study, along with representatives from Army, Navy, Marines and Air Force. Many nations from all over the world were also represented. Leaving California, I had prayed for three months about a Bible study. I wanted to continue to study God's Word. The day we moved into quarters, a young woman rode up on her bike and said, "If you need anything, let me know. My name is Pat and I am your neighbor two doors down. "Oh, by the way, God is so faithful, Billie, I have been praying for a Bible study. I attended one in Washington and it was great. It was interdenominational and I loved it. Would you be interested?"

I could not believe it.

We hugged and we talked for a few moments.

Ten minutes before we were strangers.

Two weeks later we had established a Friendship Bible Coffee, one of Stonecroft Ministries outreach programs.

Nine people came.

It grew and we multiplied.

We were only there eleven months.

Women we met at the study moved to the uttermost parts of the world and took the Light of the Gospel with them.

Light in a dark corner.

What will you do with the dark corners of your life?

They are there and they are real.

God waits for us.

Even now he's waiting for you.

Dare to believe Him. His Light is incandescent.

Night light, day light, eternal light.

"Let the hope of life give way: let the hope of God ascend."[81] St. Augustine

It will – through a praying life that shines with the Love of God.

Journal

Do you have a praying life?

What is keeping you from this discipline?

Is there a work of prayer God is calling you to do?

Prayer

Father:

How I want to praise YOUR Holy Name right now! What a powerful work YOU did in the life of Amy Carmichael. I am inspired. If YOUR way worked so long ago, it will work today because YOU are the same today, yesterday and forever. Is it possible that YOU have a work for me to do in prayer? Oh, God so many times I have failed YOU. YOU were waiting for me. I ran. YOU wanted me to be still. I wanted activity and still YOU waited. Precious Lord, I want to worship YOU and to Love YOUR presence. I want to be a woman of prayer who prays with authority – YOURS! Teach me to pray through, Savior. YOU are enough. Let my praying life shine for others through YOU.

CHAPTER NINE

A SHINING PEACE

Lead kindly light amid the encircling gloom,
Lead thou me on!
John Henry Cardinal Newman

The movie *South Pacific* held an inviting charm for me.

The island mystique grabbed me.

The thrilling music courted me.

A visit to such a place would be exhilarating, a tonic to the spirit, sunny skies, exotic flowers, and tropical evenings. Time would wrap me in a hammock from morning to night.

Pleasant breezes.

No horizon to check.

Suspended I would be, with only a touch of reality coming from monkey chatter in a coconut tree as the echo of a distant ship's horn signals its approach to the port.

I lived movies when I was young.

They allowed me to visit places I had never been and to be someone else, which was the best part. When I heard the song *Some Enchanted Evening* I knew there was a handsome stranger for me waiting somewhere. And then I heard *I'm Gonna Wash That Man Right Out Of My Hair* and I knew that was the calamity that follows such an encounter. The stirring strains of *Bali Hai* beckoned as in a distant drumbeat. A call comes to us from deep within to somewhere, some place where peace and quiet reign.

Hectic lives look for peace.

What could be better than a real rendezvous with someone you love on an island in the middle of an ocean? World War II movies were always filled with romance and danger, men and women thrown together by the tyranny of the urgent and wanting to live happily ever after! Intrigue and great, touching, moments of heroism – loss and triumph!

I loved it all!

Dark was dark, light was light.

In 1982, I had an opportunity to meet Roy in Hawaii. This was going to be about as close as I would get to my island daydream. Roy was the Air Wing Commander aboard the aircraft carrier, USS Coral Sea, and the ship was to be in Hawaii over Thanksgiving. Our daughter Kellye, 17, and our son Carey, 12, were going to stay with friends and they were as happy as could be about doing something different for a change during the holiday. We were living in San Diego. I was excited about meeting Roy somewhere remote from routine.

I had prayed about going and it appeared that the details were coming together.

I felt God had made a way for me.

I made my reservations.

I was packed to go.

Some dear friends, a Navy couple, Gary and Caroline Hughes, who were stationed at Pearl harbor, were willing to host me for a couple of days before the ship came in. I was so ecstatic over how it was all working out!

Little did I know what was brewing out in the great unknown.

My flight represented the last, predictable event of my island adventure.

We landed earlier than anticipated by 45 minutes and after standing up, ready with luggage in hand to disembark for that length of time, I discovered that we would not be getting off the plane right away.

It was Sunday and the airport personnel were short-handed and somewhat laid back; so much so, that our 747 had been directed to the wrong gate. Our plane's door would not open! They misjudged and sent us to a gate for a much smaller aircraft.

We joked about being locked aboard a 747 on the ground for an hour and a half but *it* wasn't funny,—we were!

No, it was the first of a long line of misadventures. My friend Caroline did finally meet me and we were off to her home, chatting like magpies, trying to catch up on our lives as girlfriends do. The next day was my birthday. It was a perfect day of sunshine and cool temperatures as we lunched languidly, eating a luscious pineapple salad at the strawberry pink hotel, overlooking the teal green water lapping lazily upon the beach's coastline.

Serenity was about to end.

The next morning I awakened to a strong, beating rain that had a foreboding wind lashing through heavy, low hanging clouds.

This was no ordinary rain.

Checking into the Hilton Hotel that day, I had purchased an orchid lei, which I was planning to greet my husband with as a touch of romance, just like the movies. The ship was scheduled to come in the following morning. Word came from the television that night, "For the first time in forty years a hurricane is heading for Hawaii!"

The hurricane was christened Eva.

Everyone was trying to figure out what to do.

I knew the ship would have to run away from the storm and so all my plans were on hold.

The Governor of Hawaii addressed his people that night by television.

He said, "God is releasing His wrath upon Hawaii and you need to be inside your homes by 5:00 PM." We were then told to prepare by getting food and water for ourselves and to be ready for a long arduous night.

Yes, I reminded myself, I had prayed about this trip, the planning of it and the going. My children were taken care of and were secure, but apparently I might not be!

I remembered at that moment a theme found in the book, *Walking on Water*, by writer Madeleine L' Engle. The book discussed how the life of God is in everything, how He brings "Cosmos from

Chaos."[82] Our Creator God is the great giver of life, creativity, order and destiny. The flow of life is given to us in the midst of chaos for we are His instruments.

How true.

How profound.

I was about to enter chaos.

The hotel paired each one of us Navy wives with another. You know, safety in numbers. I was housed with the senior Medical Officer's wife. She was the only strong Christian that I knew there. She lived in Camarillo, California. We both attended Bible Study Fellowship classes. Mine was in Escondido, California.

> We had a bond.

> It was our faith.

> God put us together.

"The test of discipleship is obedience to the light when truths are brought to the conscious mind."[83] God knew us and would be with us.

.

She was a part of my cosmos.

We fortified ourselves with macadamia nuts, pineapple juice and prayer and began to pray through the storm.

> We prayed for our families back on the mainland who we knew would be anxious and worried.

> We prayed for skill and safety for our men who were navigating in the storm trying to batten down airplanes and ride it out.

> We prayed for ourselves because we were afraid. We wanted to be cleansed of anything that would hinder our prayer. I remember saying, "Lord, you said in your word that you would save a whole town if you could find one righteous man. Well, we are women and we are here. We are yours. Save us, we pray."

A prayer completely trusting God in such a time can only come from a peace wrought from trial and positioned in deep trust.

When trials come, "You can complain, rebel, compromise, or run away. Or you can experience the joy, comfort, and rest that comes to disciples who keep their eyes on the prize not the pain."[84]

This was the time to keep our eyes on the prize, on Jesus.

He heard our prayer.

An unthinkable thing happened –

We fell asleep in a hurricane.

"The great word of Jesus to his disciples is abandon."[85]

We had abandoned our fear.

We gave it to Him.

"You will keep in perfect peace him whose mind is steadfast, because he trusts in you."[86]

Sleeping during a raging storm.

That's peace.

The first light of morning began shining into our room, stealing its way after a night of monumental waves pounding the beaches. At least that is what we were told. You see, we didn't hear any of it. I shouted to my friend, "Wake up, wake up, I can't believe it. We've slept through the hurricane!"

The marvelous morning light was first a layer of soft, azure blue stretching itself out along the sky and blended by a delicious apricot hue that mingled into a soft baby pink. In seconds, the bright, early shine of the sun peeked over the myriad of color and waved at the new day that was waiting.

I could not comprehend that we had slept through a storm of such magnitude! There were reports of fifty-foot waves on one of the islands. Restaurants and businesses were closed indefinitely.

We had peace.

It was given to us.

Peace is a promise to the righteous.

Damages were being assessed, power lines were down and there were outages everywhere. People were struggling to repair and move on.

Chaos was apparent.

The white sandy beaches were now blackened with debris, but the dawn had righted the bleak night once again. Clean up had begun on all the islands and makeshift lodging, lines for food and water were in the courtyard of our hotel. People gathered around outdoor grills. There had been reports of injuries, but miracle of miracles – no loss of life.

What an answer to prayer!

The phone rang, and I was told that because of the thirty-foot swells occurring in the ocean after such a storm, the ship would not be in. I said, "I believe it will come in some time today. God has brought us through this storm and I think we will see our husbands." At 11 o'clock we got the word that the carrier indeed was coming in.

No electricity!

No hot rollers!

No coffee!

No freshly pressed clothes!

We dressed looking like characters in Gilligan's Island but took our orchid leis in hand and made our way to the pier. Bedraggled but blessed, we were, searching the crowd for our husband's faces.

What a moment when a carrier comes into port! Ominous and proud. The men are standing on the deck in formation. I was hoping that my hot-pink, crumpled, awning-striped skirt would help Roy spot me and that he would not notice that I was not as put together as I usually try to be.

He found me and he didn't seem to notice my disheveled look. I was so happy to see him! I placed my flowers around his shoulders and we embraced.

God gave us such a sweet, shining moment.

We spent two more days in port, and in one of the first shops to reopen, Roy found a brass plaque that had these words of Victor Herbert engraved, "He who would learn to pray, let him go to sea." My husband had lived that one out first-hand in this experience. Being in a hurricane at sea would cause you to understand how small you are and how big God is. We bought this little treasure and even to this day it is a reminder of God's Hand of protection upon us. Thanksgiving day arrived and as the dawn made its appearance,

I heard guitar music wafting up from the beach to our hotel floor. They were having a service outside our window. People had gathered together to thank God. Strains of *Amazing Grace* were being strummed and sung.

I walked to the window, sang with them and worshipped God.

It was a holy sound, listening to people sing after the chaos of a storm. My God's Light had broken through once again into our lives and peace reigned in our thankful hearts as the fantasy of a romantic adventure that we planned became a reality of God's orchestrating love, drawing us once again to TRUST. The guardian of our souls had shined his peace upon us one more time. We all have storms to get through. In Christ Jesus – every time – His cosmos reigns.

Storms are a part of God's trials for us. In the eye of a hurricane is stillness. When it passes, it is a devastating whirlwind. In our lives there has to be a center that we operate from and that is the result of choice.

Our God should be our center.

Do we look at the impossible circumstance or do we focus on a God of impossibility? Thomas R. Kelly refers to this center as " the Shekinah of the soul."[87] It is the conscious turning to the place of God within where His Light equips us for life outwardly. After all, He comes to live within our hearts, our lives, if we have invited Him to do so.

"How do we lay hold of that life? By quiet, persistent practice in turning of all our being, day and night, in prayer and inward worship and surrender, toward Him who calls in the deeps of our souls."[88] So, we can learn by practice to do this. Then we are prepared for the storm even if we are not aware of it consciously, because we have been centered in Him.

The investments of our lives prepare us for our storms. What is inside is birthed in crisis.

Watchman Nee knew how to deal with the storms of persecution because he was centered. Imprisoned for fourteen years, he chose to live out his Christian faith in China regardless of the barriers placed upon him by the existing regime. When I read his life's story and saw the strength of his resolve, I was changed.

Watchman Nee's accusers wanted him to renounce Christianity. Communism was rampant and his organizing of house churches was an offense to the state government. But he had made a decision a long time ago that he would proclaim His God.

He did.

He would love and worship his God.

He did.

He would trust his God.

He did.

The word of God was real to him. Mentored by an English lady named Margaret Barber, he was challenged to be a man of the Cross.

Jesus did not defend himself against darkness.

Watchman would not do so either.

A story was told of an experience in prison. He had been beaten that day but no blood had come forth and he was thankful. Pulling himself up to rest upon his arm, he took a deep and grateful breath to his God. That evening, in a rich baritone voice, he began to sing his song about the Jesus. As his baritone voice carried across the courtyard of the prison, the presence of God was released. Other cellmates listened and were strengthened as a prisoner worshipped God in the midst of adversity, which is exactly what he wanted them to do. A guard stopped by to speak with him. The guard began to question him about what he was singing.

In fact, he said, "I fear you are dying."[89]

I suppose singing about God while you are incarcerated because of your God probably doesn't make much sense to one who has no God.

Watchman said, "He will not let me come home before you believe."[90]

Then the guard talked about his wife begging him to pay no attention to Pastor Nee, but every time there was opportunity, Watchman used his witness and spoke to this young jailer. Watchman's witness had good effect: "Pastor, your words are like a hammer. What must I do to be saved?"[91]

Oh, the power of a life so centered in truth that nothing dissuades it!

> No threat,

> No boundary,

> No darkness.

That was the impact of his life. Watchman Nee knew his God and today thousands worship Jesus Christ in China because of the life and work of a shining faith reflecting the absolute trust found in a sustaining Savior.

Today we face storms of divorce, financial reversal, illness, misunderstanding, abuse, and horror. The darkness of the storm cannot break us if we are centered in the Everlasting Light of God, for then we become the strong and the resolute.

The escapes that we dream of aren't real. They rarely come true except in the movies. Island life does have storms.

The encounters that God brings are life giving. We can expect them every day.

We need storms.

Years ago, I heard conference speaker, Bobbi Evans, use the term, "raining training." Cosmos in chaos.

Light is always breaking through.

His cosmos is shining.

JOURNAL

Do you view storms as opportunities for your faith to be expanded or just a fluke to endure?

Have you trained your eye to focus your faith in the midst of the crisis?

Ask yourself these questions:
>What did I learn in that whirlwind?
>Did I find God's peace?

Thank God for your growth right now.

PRAYER

Father:

Every day we need YOU to break in and birth cosmos into our chaos. We make our plans and then YOU rearrange them in order to help us trust YOU. YOU desire good for us and YOU can bring us truth in so many creative ways. Always when YOU are centered in our lives there is peace and it is profoundly from YOU because YOU are Peace. Help us to recognize when YOUR Light is breaking through so we can praise YOU and grow our trust more and more. Then our lives will reflect YOUR shining Peace.

CHAPTER TEN

CONTINUING EVER BRIGHTER

Be near me when my light is low.
Alfred Lord Tennyson

Continuing involves memory.

In April of 2000, I planted a memory in my garden. My friend Judy had sent a check to me accompanied by a note that said, "Buy something to plant in your garden in memory of your dad."

What a great idea.

So I did.

I planted a blue hydrangea bush.

Dad always tried to grow them and couldn't. You know, once they take root, they are uncontrollable. But they are temperamental in the early stages and this one proved true to the test. I envisioned the huge "snow ball" flowers that are like a small nose gay for a little girl's hand.

Plants struggle like we do.

Gardeners must have vision.

Considered old fashioned, the hydrangea has made a comeback in the past few years. It would be a welcome addition to the little English garden out back. Mine is a shade-garden filled with lacy autumn fern and pastel azaleas of pinks nestled under the full foliage of maple, pear and plum trees. Hostas emerge every spring and spread their arms like graceful fans. There are only a few spots for sun, so there has to be careful thought and planning concerning what to put in those coveted places where the light breaks through just enough to cause blooming.

Gardeners should know their garden.

I found it and placed a rustic garden cross to hang on the fence just above.

A small altar.

A large memory.

Life begins in a garden.

Sometimes, without warning, a sudden summer thunderstorm swirls in and wrecks everything. Tree branches are severed. Water pools in the lower areas.

Petunias are beaten down.

Pansies are prostrate.

Roses are limp.

Sometimes the critters of the garden dig it up. Newly planted heather is uprooted by squirrels or larger nocturnal visitors who scavenge the flowerbeds, leaving tracks and holes in the dirt.

Early morning light reveals the culprit.

It is a raccoon family on a hunt.

Sometimes you get a surprise.

A flower you did not plant peeks up through the soil and winks at you.

A serendipity.

A gift from the wind – or a bird, no doubt.

Whenever calamity befalls the garden, a true gardener continues.

God gave us gardens so we would learn how to continue.

The heart of the gardener knows there will be other seasons and fresh ideas to interpret in the garden.

The work must continue.

Preparation of the soil, seed, fertilization, pruning, disease control, water, sunlight, shade, blooming – the cycle of growth and the cycle of life.

It is his vision for the garden.

His know-how and intention cause him to continue year after year.

There is always a plan.

It is our God who nourishes our hearts, shining His light within us, causing us to continue after calamity.

"For God who said, 'Let light shine out of darkness,' made his light shine in our hearts to give us the light of the knowledge of the glory in the face of Christ."[92]

Small calamities prune us from vain victories.

I remember reading for the role of Emily in the play, *Our Town*. It was to be a citywide event in Memphis and all aspiring young actors and actresses from the surrounding schools wanted to be a part of it. My dear friend Nancy also read for the part.

I wanted it.

She got it.

I went to see the play.

She was tremendous. That role was meant for her. She even looked like I pictured Emily.

God knew I needed redirection.

I had lost my Compass.

A moving performance by my friend.

A special friendship still intact, built on mutual respect.

I continued.

When setbacks come, what we have invested in comes forth.

"Remember the wonders he has done."[93]

How do we remember Him?

We can remember Him by what we glean through calamity.

His Word tells us to abide in Him.

His Word is Truth.

His promises shine through His Word ever brighter in calamity.

We can continue.

"As the branch cannot bear fruit of itself, unless it abides in the vine, neither can you, unless you abide in me."[94]

The world does not want us to continue.

"We think, if you curled your hair, you would not look half bad, " said a feisty redhead to me, the kid who had just joined in the middle of the school year.

I did, but it didn't work any wonders in the people department. Being a ten-year old, this was a trauma.

A child's memory.

"Billie, it is impossible for you to make an "A" in chemistry. You don't have understanding."

I did make an "A" – but I still didn't understand chemistry.

A teacher's challenge.

"Mother, this house is a mess with all these boxes to unpack. I miss Dad and Kellye not being here to help us. What are we going to do?" said Carey, our son, who was twelve years old at the time. We had just moved cross-country from California, stopping in Memphis to enroll Kellye in the University of Memphis. Then he and I drove to Virginia to get settled once again. Roy was returning from a round-the-world cruise on the aircraft carrier USS Coral Sea. We had sold a house in California and relocated by ourselves – without Roy, for the first time.

"We are going to cry, pray and get better, son, because we are not alone; God is with us."

An adult's trust.

We did and we continued.

Experiences shape us and sensitize our hearts.

"God said,

Never will I leave you;

Never will I forsake you.

The Lord is my helper;

I will not be afraid.

What can man do to me?"[95]

Do we believe His Word?

If we do we can continue.

We must.

When Dayna Curry and Heather Mercer were prisoners in Afghanistan, they believed God was in their midst and they held to His Word.

Dayna read, " Blessed is the man who perseveres under trial, because when he has stood the test, he will receive the crown of life that God has promised to those who love him, James 1:12. This verse touched my heart. When I read it, I saw that the only require-ment for receiving the crown of life was that I love God. If I could just come out of the prison experience loving and worshipping God, then I would be rewarded with a crown. God was only asking me to continue loving him."[96]

She did.

Heather did.

They both continued.

The will to go on or go through can show up in the most practical and commonplace ways.

My mother, Frances, decided to made her famous homemade coconut cake this Christmas. It's quite an undertaking.

Fresh coconuts, warmed in the oven, peeled and grated, start the process. The milk is then heated on the stove with sugar and cooked until it drips off the spoon. A white seven-minute frosting is prepared in an iron skillet and set aside. The three cake layers made of the purest ingredients are baked and cooled. The assembly is done in order...a cake layer, cooled milk mixture poured over each layer, frosting and fresh coconut.

This is repeated three times.

It is a delectable confection, which can only be described as a labor of love – truly the food of angels! It has been two years since my father's death. He always helped her with the cake. We looked forward to it every year. Two and one half years later, mother baked the cake for us.

She continued.

There will be times we are asked to give all to continue.

"God is God. If He is God, He is worthy of my worship and my service. I will find rest nowhere but in His will, and that will is infinitely, immeasurably, unspeakably beyond my largest notions of what He is up to." Words written by Elisabeth Elliot in 1981 as she looked back on the events of January 6, 1956.[97]

A group of young men were brought together for a special mission, to bring the Gospel to the Aucas, a savage tribe in Ecuador – and known as killers.

Each of the young men had been set apart by God.

Jim Elliot and Pete Fleming began the work. They were joined by Nate Saint, the Missionary Aviation Fellowship pilot, Ed MCCully and Roger Youderian. Years of seeking God and preparation had come together. And God called the wives of these men as well. There was Marj, who worked the radio, alongside Nate, Barbara, Marilou, Elisabeth and Olive. They each had a heart for the mission and worked beside their husbands daily. Children were a part of these lives and so were ordinary days of meals, laundry and care for homes, simple and primitive. They also had met and talked about the possible consequences of such a mission – widowhood.

You see, God had positioned reality in them.

Events began to unfold.

There had been gift drops over the Auca clearing named "Palm Beach" for several weeks – kettles, colorful buttons, ribbon streamers, T-shirts and machetes.

All was done to open the way for relationship.

There was much prayer and seeking God to know when.

On December 18, the pilot Nate penned these words, which reflected the heart of the group in one accord. "May we who know Christ hear the cry of the damned as they hurtle headlong into a Christless night without ever a chance…. May we shed tears of repentance for these we have failed to bring out of darkness…. May God give us a new vision of His will concerning the lost and our responsibility. Would that we could comprehend the lot of these Stone Age people who live in mortal fear of ambush on the jungle trail…those who think all men in the world are killers like themselves. If God would grant us the vision, the word sacrifice would disappear from our lips…. Lord, God, speak to my own heart and give me to know Thy Holy will and the joy of walking in it."[98]

On January 6, they sang a hymn, prayed and kissed their families goodbye.

They never returned.

The wives requested to be flown over the site where the five men had been found slain. They were buried on the strip of beach. As the plane passed over this hallowed bit of earth, they knelt and prayed at the airplane windows, committing their husbands into the Arms of God Almighty.

Martyred on earth.

The work continued.

In time, Elisabeth, Marj, Barbara and Marilou made plans to return, to evangelize the tribe who took the lives of each of their husbands.

They continued.

Auca's lives were changed forever.

There was cost.

The women paid it because they chose to continue.

They were given vision, knowledge and the will to persevere.

New life was birthed where the seeds of hatred and violence were sown.

Seedlings of Hope and possibility bloomed ever brighter because of their sacrifice.

A garden of Love grew up where weeds had choked out life.

They had a Compass.

Direction.

The Master Gardener saw the persistence of their hands and was pleased.

"Today, I was troubled with the noise in my life. I was even more troubled when I saw that my beautiful corn had fallen down in a storm last night. Futilely,I tried to brace it up, but each time I tried, it fell again.

In despair I retreated, leaving the corn to its end: the compost bin. But then,When I looked at the stalks the next morning, the tips were turning up to the light. . .

. . . If I reach for the Light, You will lift me up as You did the tips of the corn."[99]

A seed dies.

Life emerges.

Struggle, will, continuance.

God's Light breaks through once again.

Stronger Life.

Every time we choose to continue after calamity, our path grows ever brighter with the shining of God's Love.

We must remember His Love and continue.

"We are not always sure where the horizon is. We would not know 'which end is up' were it not for the shimmering pathway of light falling on the white sea. The One who laid earth's foundations and settled its dimensions knows where the lines are drawn. He gives all the light we need for trust and obedience."[100]

Are you ready to continue?

It is a choice.

JOURNAL

What calamity has come that is suffocating your life?

Have you surrendered it to God?

Can you continue?

PRAYER

Father:

I put my trust in YOU. Who have I but THEE? Who orders my life and gives me the desire to follow YOU? YOU are my God. I will serve YOU and walk the narrow road. Cause me to continue because there will be enough light. I see that I must go through and YOU will be waiting every time. Waiting here on earth…waiting in Heaven. I will leave the details with YOU; just give me the courage to believe. Increase my faith and let me bring someone else along with me. Praise the Name of the Most High God who lives and reigns over all nations and whose heart is for lost people. Forgive me for forgetting. Keep me on the path that is ever brighter for YOUR Glory. I choose to continue.

CHAPTER ELEVEN
SUSTAINING EVER BRIGHTER
There are two ways of spreading light
To be the candle or the mirror that reflects it.
Edith Wharton

An Affair to Remember is my favorite romantic movie. Far removed
from today's concept of the word "affair," it is the beautifully sensitive love story of two people whose lives are changed forever when
they meet at sea on an ocean voyage.

Neither is a perfect candidate for marriage.

Cary Grant, a handsome and charming playboy, has never done an
honest day's work. Stunning Deborah Kerr, a professional singer,
has embraced art, literature and travel as a means of preparation for
marriage to a wealthy man.

The characters of Nicky (Cary Grant) and Terry (Deborah Kerr),
engaged to other people, are headed for a dramatic encounter with
destiny.

Two very poignant scenes revealing true character impact the audience.

The first involves looking at the past.

An ocean liner pulls into an enchanting place on the Riviera. The
precious French grandmother of "Nicola", as she calls him, lives in
an exquisitely breathtaking chateau overlooking the Mediterranean
Sea. Nicky takes Terry ashore to meet his very dear grandmother,
Janeau. Rarely seeing her international grandson, she is wonderfully
surprised. Every day she can be found praying in the chapel built
for her by her late husband. As she opens the door and steps outside, they are waiting for her. Surrounded by artistry in every sense,
antiques, fine paintings and endearing gardens, Janeau's life is
ordered.

The very air she breathes is delicate with the scent of beauty.

Her husband was an Ambassador and she, a former concert pianist.

Nicky asks her to play for Terry.

Fragile arthritic hands, that miss a note or two, reluctantly touch the
keyboard.

Charming Terry begins to sing in a lilting, rich mezzo-soprano voice the words, in French, to the piece, *A Love Affair.*

And One begins.

Wistful eyes meet.

Inviting smiles are exchanged.

Love is born.

In this moment, the loveliness of Terry's character draws Nicky to her.

Grandmother knows they were destined to be together.

Nicky and Terry now know they are in love.

How will this Love Affair work out?

Once they are back aboard ship, a plan is launched.

Each will work for six months and then rendezvous at the top of the Empire State Building on a certain date.

He will go back to the one skill he let go of long ago – painting.

She will go back to the one she knows – singing.

An untimely automobile accident occurs the day they are to meet.

Crippled and unable to walk, her life with a wheel chair begins.

She misses the appointment and decides to forever remain out of his life unless she can walk. He is devastated at her "no show" but tries to fill his life with painting. Months later at the theatre, in a chance meeting, they see each other for the first time since the day of broken promise.

Unrequited love awakens.

Finding where she lives, he drops by unannounced to bring her the gift of a lace shawl; a present from Janeau, who is now deceased. They begin to reconstruct what has taken place in their lives since the boat adventure.

He is now a successful painter.

She now teaches music at a school for children.

He does not know about the wheel chair.

As Nicky prepares to leave, he suddenly remembers the gift.

Janeau wanted Terry to have the lace shawl.

Terry receives it and tenderly drapes it upon her shoulders.

His eyes gaze upon the picture before him of Terry wearing Janeau's lace shawl.

She looks exactly as he painted her.

It was this painting that established him as an artist.

Nicky relates the story of a young, handicapped woman in a wheel chair who came into the art gallery and admired the painting but had no money.

Since she was poor, the painting was given to her.

An instantaneous awareness moves over his body.

Terry sees what is happening and her heart starts to pound.

Light is breaking through at last.

Realization and possibility embrace.

Nicky looks around the room and then immediately rushes into her bedroom.

He sees the painting, the wheel chair and the truth.

This second scene is the resolution of the story.

As he sweeps her up into his arms and questions why she did not reveal the truth, she explains the circumstances and says, "Don't cry, darling. If you can paint, I can walk."

In a flash, we, the audience, understand their sacrifice.

It is an exceptional insight, a revelation of true love.

Two people meant to be together.

The character of love shined.

Cost, perseverance, triumph.

I weep every time I see the movie – even though I know when the lines are coming.

Why?

Because, the human spirit is moved by such purity in relationship.

I want to share two love stories of real people who have led amazing lives of commitment and triumph in the midst of adversity.

It was the Love of God that brought them together.

It was the Love of God that held them when severe tests came.

It is the Love of God that bears witness to lives sustained through suffering.

God's Love always triumphs.

It shines EVER BRIGHTER.

He is the author.

"Who are these coming to the sacrifice?"[101]

In 1962, Marolyn Ford, a young, blind woman, married Acie Ford, an eager new minister of the Gospel. Acie prayed every night for ten years that God would restore Marolyn's sight. At age 18, she was diagnosed at Mayo Clinic with macular degeneration. Every evening, they would kneel beside their bed and pray for the healing of Marolyn's sight.

That prayer was answered August 26, 1972.

When Acie finished praying, Marolyn opened her blue eyes and for the first time saw her beloved Acie.

"Acie, I can see! I can see!" she shouted.

Marolyn could see.

Marolyn could read.

She was tested at the doctor's office.

Medically she was still blind.

BUT Marolyn could see.

God had given her a miracle.

For two decades, Marolyn spoke around the world telling of God's healing Hand upon her life. She loved His Word and loved the ministry He had given to her.

"The commands of the Lord are radiant, giving light to the eyes."[102]

She was radiant with God and she could see His Light! Her book, *These Blind Eyes Now See*, recounts this miracle.

A fall in a bathtub in 1991 changed her life again.

Numbness and pain followed.

More testing revealed a crushed bone in the lower spine.

Surgery followed and so did more falling and more tests.

In 1992, she was diagnosed with an autonomic neuropathy disorder.

The digestive system was shutting down. Her body could not digest or eliminate food.

Fear came.

Now, real suffering entered her life.

Perseverance infused her soul with iron.

Faith to endure was given by her Heavenly Father and the book *Grace To Endure* was birthed at this time.

She believed in miracles.

She had been given one.

Now the greater miracle of an enduring grace would be upon her life.

For a few years, she could eat.

BUT medication had to be taken every third day in order to cleanse her system.

It was a screaming agony, but she endured.

One day this procedure no longer worked.

Marolyn stopped eating.

No food or water since the spring of 1996.

Her source of food became nutritional feeding from a tube inserted into her chest for fourteen hours a day.

Always hungry.

Muscles started to shut down.

Still she would go and share her faith when able.

Still she believed her God could heal.

Still she prayed, wept and worshipped Him.

More brokenness.

Bones crumbled but her spirit refused to give in.

The motorized scooter, her only source of mobility, had to be parked.

Unable to garden, crochet or cook, she still proclaims the sufficiency of her Lord from her hospital bed.

There is an unwavering belief in the God of her life.

She lives to praise Him.

She delights in her family, Acie, Sharon, John and the precious grandchildren.

She looks for God's smile.

The blue eyes that were blind have a heavenly look but the strong will to serve is still there.

Tomorrow if God should choose to raise her up, she'll be ready.

She lives an expectant life and beside her is a man who has cherished her.

It is a love story born from the heart of God.

Their lives have been rich with His Presence.

They live for Him.

God is holding Marolyn.

She is a mirror of His marvelous Love.

God holds her future.

Shining ever brighter, sustained through suffering.

Their story is God's.

"…Blest by faith…others will love and we will teach them how."[103]

Mark Stone was a pastor to our family twice during our Navy years, during the late 1960s and again in the late 1970s, in Virginia Beach, Virginia.

We heard Mark preach and we were hooked.

Humor, scholarship, and startling honesty.

He was real in his faith.

People know real.

You don't get God's Truth any straighter.

The first time I heard him call Joseph the "first streaker", because he lost his robe as he ran from Potiphar's wife, I knew that Mark had a keen gift of insight in the Word and relevancy to the real world.

You did not easily forget his teaching.

He challenged you to BE the Gospel to a needy world.

HE WAS.

God's imprint was on his life.

In March of 1957, Mark and Nancy were getting ready to move into married quarters for students at Baylor University. They had a little girl named Cheryl, who was a year old. Nancy and Cheryl were with friends. Mark was to join them later.

The big task ahead for him was to clean the floors in preparation for moving in.

Gasoline was suggested to Mark as an effective cleaning solvent.

That was the mistake.

An explosion occurred when the gasoline was ignited by the pilot light on the water heater.

He became a human torch.

Running out of the apartment building in flames, rolling on the grass, he committed his earthly life to God. Some neighborhood children rushed to his side; believing he was living his last moments, he shared his faith with them.

Mark thought he was going home to heaven that day.

He did not.

He was going to live, to be sustained through suffering.

His life would be a testimony to the enduring grace of God.

When Mark spoke to people who were suffering, they listened.

They knew he knew.

He was burned over sixty five percent of his body.

BUT his eyes were untouched.

Shielded.

It was as if Unseen Hands had covered them, protecting them from the flames.

They did.

How did he get out of that building?

How was he to live?

He would find out.

Many surgeries followed.

Skin grafts, healing, waiting.

God was there.

Raised up to be a minister of the Gospel with power and authority over darkness!

He recognized darkness because he had experienced it.

He knew God's Light because he lived!

He was God's mighty bearer of the Word.

Chosen to suffer.

"The unfolding of your words gives light; it gives understanding to the simple."[104]

He would laugh about now if he were reading over my shoulder because Mark's humor invaded the spiritual with common sense. He would say, "You have this one pegged, Cash; God gives understanding to the simple and that's me, simpleminded Mark."

What is profound is this: we have to be simple in order to perceive God.

The Gospel is for all men.

Mark had strong intellect but he came across with a simplicity in the Gospel that brought understanding to the child, acceptance to the streetwise, practicality to the learned and exposure to the religious.

How?

The Word of God sheds Light.

Darkness was exposed.

God's man is authentic.

God's Light shines where there is integrity in faith.

The second time we were stationed in Virginia Beach, once again we became a part of Mark's church. This time we got to know Nancy, a chosen helpmeet to her husband.

She was the love of his life, enabling him to be, to go and to do.

He was in front.

She was behind him, helping him to get ready to be in front.

An athlete at heart, Mark could still grab a tennis racket and off he and Roy would head for the court. When the Dallas Cowboys and the Washington Redskins played, a good debate was in order. Roy was a Skins fan; Mark was a Cowboys fan.

He lived on the cutting edge of life, enjoying every moment.

His life was full.

There was a successful television ministry that included his son, Jonmark, a talented musician. Because Mark believed that a strong leader should be involved in the community, he served on a variety of boards – including crime prevention, drug abuse, Fellowship of Christian Athletes, hospital chaplains and missions.

He had a voice with young people because He had a vibrant Christianity.

His laughter was raucous.

He loved to joke and people played jokes on him because he could take it.

The Gospel, however, was no laughing matter to him.

His heart was evangelism.

This body continued to suffer so much through the years and finally began to slow down, but he didn't. After serving several pastorates, he finally decided to go into full time evangelism.

On the road he went.

At that time, I dubbed him the "Rolling Stone."

It took more preparation but he gave it all he had and lives were changed forever.

He began to minister to ministers.

They loved him because they needed a Mark Stone as a friend. The 1980s came and he was diagnosed with polymiositis, a weakening and inflammation of the leg muscles.

Still he pressed on.

Pain was a part of Mark's daily life, but he never stopped serving.

Nancy equipped him to continue to run the race set before him.

Joining the staff of a local church as an associate, he still did the work of the evangelist as well as counseling.

Four heart attacks came in quick succession and other complications developed.

The body was tired.

Never in all the years we knew Mark did we ever think of him as sick. His friends loved him dearly and he had many.

He was a man who knew his God to be faithful.

Mark ran his race all the way to the end with dignity, dynamic faith and dogged assurance.

At his funeral, nine pastors paid tribute to this incredible friend, filled with laughter, housed in a broken body.

We miss him.

He and Nancy shared a love story that some only find in classic romantic movies or lines of poetry:

"Thou shalt love and be loved by, forever: a Hand
     like this hand
Shall throw open the gates of new life to thee!
See the Christ stand!"[105]

It was love born of God and sustained by His Light.

Sacrifice, cost, perseverance…and triumph.

On February 18, 2001, God held Nancy as Mark entered the shining city.

God is still holding her and she is shining EVER BRIGHTER.

Our God gave us courageous stories so we would be encouraged. We need to read about people who were sustained.

Another line from the movie, *An Affair To Remember*, that punctuates this truth says, "Winter must be cold for those who have no warm memories."

Godly marriages that position the living God in the center of their lives have warm memories when they grow old. Their Love Affair with God continually creates anew but keeps the old. Loving Him brings a shining EVER BRIGHTER on the path of the righteous.

Do you know the Love that is everlasting, eternal, unending?

If you do, you will have warm memories to keep you when winter comes.

Winter will come.

"We continually remember before our God and Father your work produced by faith, your labor prompted by love, and your endurance inspired by hope in our Lord Jesus Christ."[106]

JOURNAL

Will embracing the Word of God prepare me for suffering?

Can I trust the plans God has for me, plans for my good?

Is there someone who has mentored the Christian Life for me?

How can I be an instrument of God's Love this week to that person?

Prayer

Father:

I am in awe of YOUR Love. Oh God, I want to be pleasing to YOU. Have YOUR way in my life. I do not know what is ahead on my journey but I know YOU will be there. YOU will never leave me nor forsake me. I can go through with YOU but I can do more than go through, I can go through with acceptance and joy in YOU. It is possible because YOU have shown me the lives of people who suffered but were sustained. They lived life, loved, laughed and still gave themselves to others. As the shadows of suffering grew more ominous, they grew brighter. They were looking at YOU. YOU are the Light that caused them to shine EVER BRIGHTER. Help me to remember their example, to remember YOU. Bless YOUR Holy Name, BLESSED LIGHT.

CHAPTER TWELVE

RENEWING EVER BRIGHTER

I can again thy former light restore
William Shakespeare

Are you a keeper?

My husband Roy still has his geography notes from college stashed in the attic. We've carried them around with us through all the moves spanning thirty years of military life and almost ten years of civilian life since our Navy retirement.

Why?

He might need them.

Legible they may not be, but he's hanging on.

He's a keeper.

I still have an elegant, royal blue, satin ball gown with Lady Diana sleeves. I have had it for 17 years, during which time I've only worn it three times.

Why?

I have reasons.

I got it on sale for one third of its original cost, which means it was a bargain and I was supposed to have it.

The money I saved on the dress, I spent on the jewelry I wore with the gown.

I felt like Lady Diana when I wore it.

It is a reminder of romance, youth and the past.

I might need it again.

Dated it is, but in a timeless way and I am hanging on.

I am a keeper, too.

We keep stuff.

Sometimes there is rationale and sometimes not.

This is the time of year for me to clean out closets. I received a telephone call today with a request for clothing.

I'm getting the message.

First it is a thought.

I take a serious look.

A request comes in.

I promise to deliver.

I deliver.

Every time I do what I should do, I am renewed.

Getting rid of stuff renews me.

How is it possible that cleaning out a closet can be so beneficial to one's psyche?

Because in all of life, we hang on, when we really need to let go.

We keep, cling and hoard, when we need to give away.

We build a wall around our heart when we need to open a window to our soul so God's Light can break through.

Every time I release and let go, I am renewed.

As a child, it was my heart I safeguarded. I rushed to the secret place where my Lord and I could weep together. There was no humiliation – just love and comfort.

"For in the time of trouble he shall hide me in his pavilion, in the secret of his tabernacle shall he hide me."[107]

As a mother, it was my children that I clutched.

I bargained with God constantly.

"Lord, will you allow me the privilege of seeing my children grow up?"

He did.

But it was a process.

In the parenting years, they were such a polestar in my life.

I needed a creative tool to help me let go.

I asked God to give me one.

It was a letter.

Writing letters is something I know how to do. I don't know how many I wrote through thirty years of Navy life, but it was significant. Roy and I would throw away all the letters written on a particular cruise in anticipation of homecoming. He threw his into the ocean on the way home. It was a kind of ceremonial and picturesque way of saying "This part is over. We made it."

Letters are personal.

Words written from the heart about love, life and longing are family treasures.

I have kept our courtship letters in an antique ottoman and one day, our children will know the kind of love we had from the beginning, from our own words.

I needed to write my children some letters of release.

Not because they needed it.

Because I did.

For each of them I wrote a letter when they graduated from high school, heading for college. Kellye graduated in 1983 from high school in Southern California and enrolled in Memphis State University in the fall. Roy was overseas and due back from a round-the-world cruise on the USS Coral Sea in September in Virginia. The day I gave Kellye her letter, Carey and I were to drive from Tennessee to Virginia to relocate. We cried so hard the first few miles that I could barely drive and then we hit a storm in the mountains and were engulfed in a heavy, darkened cloud cover. Trying to keep me focused enough to drive slowly and safely through the strong turbulent winds Carey said, "Mom, how about playing a Sandi Patti tape."

I did.

We made it to the top of the mountain in an unrelenting summer rain with God's music guiding our thoughts.

God's light literally broke through in the clouds and in our hearts.

We had said goodbye to a season of Kellye's life.

We missed her already.

The letter was an affirmation of her life, filled with thoughts of looking back and then looking ahead.

It was a letting go and an embracing of the future.

Carey graduated in 1988 from high school in Virginia Beach, Virginia. I wrote a similar letter, carefully placing it into his duffel bag. He was going to The Citadel, a Military College in Charleston,

South Carolina. I thought he'd find it immediately, but it was Christmas before he found it. I must have hidden it well.

Roy and I drove him to school, said goodbye and then drove home to Virginia Beach.

I wept all the way home.

It is a seven-hour trip.

That's a long cry.

Writing brought release.

I also wrote letters when their weddings came.

Another rite of passage.

A hope, joy, thanksgiving and a prayer for each new addition to our lives.

God gave Todd to Kellye and Charity to Carey.

Then He gave them back to us – with interest!

Eight grandchildren are the legacy of the Cash/Hall, Cash/Sheppard, Cash/ Ellis renewal plan. Each one brought new life.

Fathers and daughters,

Mothers and sons.

Fathers give the bigger picture to their children.

They give vision.

They let go.

Mothers are the nurturers.

They instinctively hang on.

The Bible tells us that a man shall leave his family and become one flesh with his wife.

God knew that sons had to have a special mandate in scripture so their mothers would let go!

Sons are heads of families.

Mothers need to release sons to daughters-in-law.

No one ever talks about this mysterious transition. There is only one woman in a marriage and it is the wife.

I had prayed for my children's mates and God had chosen the best.

Kellye's wedding was exciting to anticipate and plan.

She had everything meticulously organized.

She's a planner and she was ready.

When July 8, 1989 came and went, I felt great contentment. Her wedding had been exquisite and filled with fun and festivity. Handsome Todd was smiling but had tears in his eyes when he saw her come down the aisle. It was so touching.

There was an acknowledged peace and release.

I did feel the same on the day of Carey and Charity's wedding, but I had to do some emotional homework to get there.

Why was it easy for me with Kellye but hard for me with Carey?

Fathers and daughters,

Mothers and sons.

A few days before his wedding on July 25th, 1992, I sat down and wrote what was in my heart. I read this journal piece to Charity a few years later.

With tears in her eyes, she understood about Mothers and Sons. She is the mother of three boys and two girls. Kellye has one boy and two girls.

Journal – July 16, 1992

"Oh God, I release my son into Your Hands afresh and anew today.

He has been mine exclusively for twenty-two years. I have relished the job with periods of delight and challenge and periods of anguish and exasperation.

Help me, Oh God, to see with Your Eyes once again the finished work, a young man equipped and prepared to meet life head on, to marry beautiful Charity and to grow into one as You would have them do.

Give me a new direction. Help my clutching heart to release, yes, to release and let go, to embrace the distant horizon.

Lord, You and I have never walked this way before but we have walked together through seas of calm and storms of change many times. All of my life has been preparation for the next season, next appointment, even this moment.

His passion and commitment to you are my jewels.

His pursuit of excellence was born in the furnace of adversity – training to be an athlete.

Fire does that.

His reward for purity is a Godly "Esther" that You have prepared for him.

What a joy she is.

How brief has his childhood been.

I wished I could have always known what I now know.

I've wished whole periods of my life away when I needed to LIVE MOMENTS!

Mothering doesn't last forever.

It's meant to teach us surrender from self…

> Release from possessiveness,

> To nurture for a time,

> To develop identity for the next generation.

It is fragile.

I awakened today to realize that a new door awaits him. What an exciting one!

And one awaits me too.

You are the same God for us both.

He cannot wait to walk through his door.

The light of promise is so brilliantly beautiful.

I, however, need Your Hand upon mine to stabilize my anxious, fretful heart.

Just now through the crack, I sense an unfolding, lingering light gently wooing me down an EVER BRIGHTER path.

I want to go, BUT,

I think I'll go outside first and pinch my geraniums. They need it. It'll cause them to seek the sun. When the rains come, there'll be fresh growth.

Today I felt the pinch, and the rains came and now my heart is fertile ground for the fresh seed of transition. Give me Your Grace, Oh Jesus."

HE DID.

We had a wonderful, blessed day.

It was sweet Charity who wept as she recited her vows, so tender and endearing.

Today, Carey, a father of five, serves our nation as a US Navy Chaplain.

Chaplains lead men.

Men go to war.

Mothers and wives must learn to let go.

In James Bradley's book, *Flags of Our Fathers*, we are told the story of the six young men who climbed to the top of Mount Suribachi on February 23, 1945 and raised the American Flag. They were ordinary boys from New Hampshire, Texas, Kentucky Pennsylvania, Wisconsin and Arizona. "Only two of them walked off the island. One was carried off with shrapnel embedded up and down his side. Three were buried there, so they are also a representative picture of Iwo Jima."[108]

A time of courage, risk and sacrifice in our history.

The great depression was a part of their lives and "religious faith and strong mothers."[109]

Mothers have influence.

Note how in some instances in the Old Testament, as a king is introduced, the name of his mother is identified.

"In the eighteenth year of the reign of Jeroboam, son of Nebat, Abijah became king of Judah...His mother's name was Maacah...He committed all the sins his father had done before him, his heart was not fully devoted to the Lord his God."[110]

Mothers help to define the hearts of their children.

They must develop character and then release each one to his destiny.

"Men are what their mothers made them."[111]

Always this tenable bond surfaces in literature.

The day our Flag was raised at Iwo Jima, the ships in the harbor began to sound their horns. There were shouts from troops who still had to wage the bloody battle that day but the sound that erupted was likened to New Year's Eve at Times Square in New York City.

They gave and we received.

Renewal is born out of surrender.

Surrendered lives bring honor to God.

"Perseverance keeps honor bright."[112]

Marcia and Richard Ward live in our town. Richard has had Lou Gehrig's disease for seven years. Slowly he has lost the mobility of his body as muscles have shut down. Marcia has cared for him day and night with the aid of a few wonderful nurses who have been faithful to him during his illness. No food since the spring of 1996, he is bed-ridden and is given nutritional feeding through the stomach.

He cannot speak, but Marcia understands every tiny expression. She has had to let go daily in order to be renewed by a God that knows what she must have to cope.

They both know about sacrifice.

Immobile except for the movement of cheek muscles, Richard has learned to let go.

Through the movement of these muscles and a light sensor directed toward the computer, Richard writes.

He has a keen and creative mind – and a heart for God. Although unable to speak, he is an effective communicator.

On a day I needed healing and rest because of a severe allergic reaction caused from medication, Richard e-mailed me.

I had lost my speaking voice and had a week to get restored before leaving to speak in Pennsylvania.

I was spent.

He said in the e-mail, "Billie, I know what it is like to lose your voice but the inner voice is still there. I will be praying for you."

I was healed and made ready through the prayers of others who let go and allowed God do the work through them. Richard's prayer prepared me.

We must understand that we are only renewed in letting go.

The way to renewal is relinquishment. Our rights are HIS.

I cannot store up, hang on, keep or grasp my life if I want to be renewed.

"But this one thing I do: Forgetting what is behind and straining toward what is ahead, I press on toward the goal to win the prize for which God has called me heavenward in Christ Jesus."[113]

I want a faith lift every day.

I cannot get filled up with God if my cup is not emptied.

I need to give away my trophies.

I need to rid my life of old wounds.

I need new promises to wear.

I need dreams to ponder.

I CAN.

"Forget the former things; do not dwell on the past.

See I am doing a new thing!

I am making a way in the desert."[114]

And that way is left up to our God to choose for us.

The Shepherd who leads us can make even a desert EVER BRIGHTER because of His shining Presence.

I want to experience this journey of faith.

Will you join me? Get rid of stuff. He'll show you your stuff. You will weigh less and your life will shine.

"If you repent, I will restore you."[115]

Lighter, brighter is His way.

Let go;

Let God.

Journal

What is it that you have held on to that must be released?

Do you want to be renewed?

Can God establish the plans He has for you?

Will you trust HIS plans?

Prayer

Father:

How great YOUR Vision for my life is. How small is mine. I have spent many years gathering stuff. I need to let go. I need to give all of it to YOU. I do not know what is around the next bend, Oh Lord, but I know Who is. I have been encumbered for such a long time. I need to travel lighter. Take my clutching heart and blow upon my life a fresh wind of hope, a new liberty. Transform my mind. I will walk with YOU. Let me hold my children lightly. They are YOURS. Thank YOU for the mothering/fathering years and thank YOU that I can embrace them as friends. Praise YOU for bringing others into my family. I will have enough love for each one because YOU supply us with all that we need. Overflow, Lord. Show me how to release all that I hold. They are YOURS. Praise YOU for YOUR WAYS. What a renewing God we have!

CHAPTER THIRTEEN

FOLLOWING HIS LIGHT HOME

Heaven's light shines forever
Percy Bysshe Shelley

"The path of the righteous is like the first gleam of dawn, shining ever brighter till the full light of day." Proverbs 4:18

Running the race,

The finish in sight,

Home,

At last.

All the yearning, looking, waiting now ceased.

I visualized Roy's Navy homecomings long before they arrived.

Looking back with appreciation at God's faithfulness over the many months of separation,

Cheered on by the present schedule, chock-full of details to get ready.

Hope realized.

Contemplating the future, daydreaming about what was ahead – birthdays, holidays, intimacy, relationship, goals.

Prescience,

Impatience,

High hopes,

Everything planned in minutia.

What elation to know the cruise was over.

I made it through.

Paying bills, sick kids, lonely Sundays, solo ball games, broken washers, car problems, writing letters, missed holidays, storms, drought, calendars, organizing folks, parenting, believing, praying, struggling, seeking, releasing, letting go and finally the day of homecoming arrives.

The expectancy is shining.

I am carried by an intense momentum throughout the final day.

I have a checklist and it is complete.

My house is spanking clean. It is filled with my husband's favorite foods that I have lovingly prepared. My children have made posters and decorated our home with welcome. We carry some to the pier – and it is some party.

We can't wait!

Getting dressed isn't drudgery, it is delight. Clothes have carefully been selected.

Our hearts are about to burst!

Bands are playing stirring patriotic music.

Crowds are gathering. Hundreds are on hand to cheer the ship's arrival.

Anxious faces search the horizon for the carrier, the great gray lady. As she approaches, there are whistles and shouts and tears of accomplishment.

There is no way he can miss us! He knows we are waiting for him!

In a few suspended moments we shall see him face to face.

Completion.

I have made it through.

He has come home.

Together we are home.

There are no words to describe the sense of relief, the gratitude to God, for He was there all the time with me, never leaving me, always available, constantly pushing my faith, turning it, growing it, causing it to seek HIM and now I see the reward.

It is the LIGHT found at the finish line.

Just a tiny glimpse of heaven.

A foretaste.

A prelude.

A realization.

"If I find in myself a desire which no experience in the world can satisfy, the most probable explanation is that I was made for another world."[116]

Our God is preparing a homecoming for you and me that is not on the chart of comprehension to the mind.

He has "set eternity in the hearts of men."[117]

Why don't we think about HEAVEN or talk about it once in a while as we are journeying toward it on earth?

Why don't we prepare for it as we would other events of jubilation in our lives?

Why don't we anticipate HEAVEN?

God intends to prepare us for it on earth, by how we think, how we live.

Training for holiness.

"God designed holiness to be invigorating. He intends the holy life to be an odyssey of wonder."[118]

Holy lives long for HEAVEN.

Should my relationship with Him develop a Holy life?

"But you are the ones chosen by God, chosen for the high calling of priestly work, chosen to be a holy people, God's instruments to do his work and speak out for him, to tell others of the night-and-day difference he made for you-from nothing to something, from rejected to accepted."[119]

Oh, the wonder of it!

Our journey toward it is an odyssey.

Heraclitus, the Greek poet and philosopher, said, "The soul is dyed with the color of its thoughts. Think only on those things that are in line with your principles and can bear the full light of day. The content of your character is your choice. Day by day, what you choose, what you think and what you do is who you become."

Is there anything "excellent or praiseworthy – think about such things?"[120]

Think about HEAVEN.

The holy – in Him – go to HEAVEN.

God's Full Light of Day.

I heard Elisabeth Elliot encourage her radio listeners to think about HEAVEN every day.

Why?

Because we were made for HEAVEN.

All of our life's experiences have urged us, constrained us to seek more.

HEAVEN is MORE.

When the earthly race is over, you're done.

It is a good feeling to be finished.

A sense of reward lingers for a moment.

But is that all there is?

Not for the believer!

The finish is finalized in Full Light.

JESUS is "your very great reward."[121]

Forever to be in His Presence.

That's Home.

Looking toward heaven every day will change life on earth.

Choice changes.

HEAVEN is full light.

As I write this chapter, I am a guest visiting in a luxurious log home that exudes comfort and warmth; the home is situated on a rugged pastoral mountain in Pennsylvania.

It is known as Jack's Mountain, a part of the Allegheny chain. This morning, as I sit cocooned in comfortable clothes on the screened porch, I feel cloistered away from the clatter of life. Such tranquility certainly restores.

"Lord, I want to hear from You."

I hear the crackle of the wind as it whips through the rustling trees and the sounds of rushing water recklessly spilling over rocks and terrain, down hill from a mountain stream.

"You are here, Lord."

Nature shouts Your existence.

Stillness, rest, refreshment.

Basking in the love of God – satisfied, contented.

Just a touch of heaven on earth.

I don't want to leave.

I want to stay, but tomorrow I must leave for I have work to do down in the valley.

I have been pondering HEAVEN today, reading about it in God's Word.

I am asking God to show me a picture of HEAVEN from His Word.

I discover in scripture that it will be a place of "no more night."[122]

"The city has no need of the sun or of the moon to shine upon it, for the glory of God has illumined it, and its lamp the Lamb."[123]

Wow, no more night!

I will walk on streets of pure gold, the very commodity for which people work their whole lives, accruing as much as they can on this earth.[124]

Don't you find it pointlessly futile that we spend so much time on earth striving for wealth?

We will walk on gold there.

It will be under our feet.

The foundation is laid with precious stones, the gates are each a single pearl.[125]

Beauty.

Luminous beauty.

"The redeemed heart hungers for beauty."[126]

There will be all kinds of treasure in Heaven.

"You will have Tony as a treasure.

Tony…I don't remember any Tony who would be a treasure.

Tony, the older man you witnessed to on your first job, while you were still a teenager in

New York City.

Tony's in heaven.

He's a treasure.

There's the treasure of another man who tenderly cared for his wife in old age, during the ten years she was totally paralyzed.

There's her treasure of an uncomplaining grateful spirit.

There's the treasure of purity – a teenager who kept himself from the world's stain.

There's the treasure of an IMPORTANT MAN who remained meek in all his relationships.

There is the treasure of parents who were faithful in raising their children, sacrificing their own independence and gratification for them.

Almost limitless treasures for people in HEAVEN."[127]

What abundance, what fortune, what a storehouse to look forward to as God's children.

HEAVEN houses riches.

I read that all my prayers have been kept in golden bowls and have been offered as incense to my Lord.[128]

Incredible.

Could I have prayed more?

How precious to envision what HEAVEN will be like.

My prayers were not wasted and neither were yours.

They worked the will of God on earth and they were an aroma of love to Him.

I learn that the saints of God will be gathered together in fellowship from the nations.[129]

There will be true worship around The Throne of the Lamb of God![130]

Hands lifted up in adoration, faces seeking His Face.

What a privilege.

Surely we will all have work to do.

"And His bond-servants shall serve Him; and they shall see His face, and His name shall be on their foreheads."[131]

What we have done on earth will have equipped us for our service in HEAVEN.

We shall take our knowledge of Jesus to HEAVEN and we shall grow in our knowledge of Him.

"God will have productive work for us to do. We will increase our knowledge of Him."[132]

Why?

Because He has lived in our hearts on earth and now we will live in His Presence forever.

Scripture tells us that it will be a place of no more pain.[133]

No more tears[134]

No more death[135]

No abominations[136]

No needs[137]

Struggle ceased forever.

The saint is Home.

How glorious it will be.

Today as I reflect on it, I am reminded of an incident that occurred when I was a nine-year old child. My paternal grandmother, Mama Bella was suffering from cancer and we were called to the old farm in Burnsville, Mississippi. I can still see the little den as people crowded in to comfort the family. She had fought an intense battle. Her will was so impenetrable. Mama Bella was a schoolteacher who had taught five grades in a one-room schoolhouse.

She wanted to live.

She prayed to live.

As I went into her room, the atmosphere was suffocating, horrid. The reality of death hung heavy, but she was singing hymns and so I came alongside and tried to join her. Together we sang.

I did not always know all the words but I knew they were about Jesus.

Mama Bella was going home.

Suddenly she sat up in the bed and her eyes were wide open and bright with light and exclaimed, "Doc, I see you son, I see you. Mother is coming…. It won't be long now." Then she collapsed and fell back upon the bed.

It wasn't long.

Mama Bella saw into HEAVEN!

Her beloved son, Billy, was there. I was named after him. Doc was his nickname and his untimely death at age fourteen from an accidental gunshot is what brought her to Jesus.

As a child I experienced the reality of HEAVEN that day.

As an adult, today God brought it back to my remembrance.

Looking back, I see that God's plan for you and me was always the best.

A unique journey for each individual life.

He knew us.

Personalities, strengths, weaknesses, hopes, dreams.

He had to get us ready for Heaven.

Now the great revelation is this: HE IS ALL WE HAVE EVER NEEDED.

Were the promises to the righteous proven true?

A resounding YES!

Looking back, I can now see the evidence of His provision.

I came into His Light out of the darkness of my own sin.

Jesus was the way.

His Light began to illuminate my path daily and His Words were the road signs – my map to life and now to the City of Light, the Holy City.

What were they?

He was always present.[138]

He examined my life daily.[139]

He made me secure.[140]

He gave me blessing and favor.[141]

He brought deliverance to me.[142]

As I believed and acted upon these truths, my life began to "shine like stars" with His Love and Sufficiency.[143]

I learned obedience.

I began to grow and yearn for more of Him.

My passion was turned toward His Heart, His pursuits.

I loved His Presence more than my own.

Prayer unto Him was breath to me.

His life became mine.

Peace prevailed so completely that nothing else could move or shake my foundation.

My trust was nailed down to HIM ALONE.

I trusted His Timing

Looking back, His Light was there.

But there was MORE – a shining Ever Brighter, yet to come.

People I read about in books and people I met in life began to live out before me His Light, and my path opened even more.

His way works.

It worked for them.

It worked for me.

I saw calamity come and go.

I continued.

Others had.

Their success encouraged me.

I saw the revelation of a loving God who sustained His own in suffering all the way to the end. He always reveals Himself in suffering.

He revealed Himself to me.

I saw that I had to relinquish all my rights and learn to let go of EVERYTHING but HIM.

Letting go brought Liberty – real Life because of His Light.

I remembered.

PhilipYancy reminded me of this need to remember.

"Remembering my relationship with God takes effort and intentionality. I cannot pull out a home video and watch our history together and growth together. There are no photo albums of living in faith. I must consciously work out reviewing both the progress of the ache and the progress of the healing."[144]

And guess what?

I did.

And God was there all along that path.

In the book of Revelation this Light that guided me throughout my earthly journey is finally identified. He is called the Daystar – The Bright Morning Light.

Brilliantly arrayed before us.

Transcendent Light.

Majesty manifested.

Holy, Holy, Holy.

And we are invited to "The marriage supper of the Lamb."[145]

We shall be dressed in white linen.[146]

Great multitudes will be shouting praises to Him.[147]

What a celebration.

Awesome worship,

Awed saints,

Awe inspiring opportunities given to us to bring gifts to Him. Some have crowns to cast before Him, to lay down as an offering.[148]

Will you?

Will I?

What have we done along the way for others because of His great love to us?

Have we loved Him more than ourselves?

What might He consider as worthy in our lives?

The souls of people to whom we have given His Truth…

The times we extended kindness to a stranger because of our love for Jesus…

The songs lifted to Him in praise, inviting and strengthening us to go and be the body of Christ to a wounded world…

The invitation to give money sacrificially to send others to mission fields ripe for harvest…

The prayer uttered for a struggling, anguished heart…

The leap out of our comfort zone when He stretched us to lead, not follow…

The surrendering of our rights with gladness to His wishes…

What will be our crown?

It was then I turned and heaven's reality swept over me like a gentle unsuspecting breeze after a stifling hot summer's day.

God's Light broke through.

I had understanding.

I saw.

The journey is about Him.

It's about weaning us from our ways to embrace His Purpose.

Loving people to Him.

He cares about people. And they will be there from every race and every generation in history.

Babies, children and old people,

Presidents and peasants,

Rich and poor,

Distinguished and obscure,

Diverse, but devoted to The King of Kings.

We will recognize many.

They will recognize you and me because we are the family of God.

The Daystar will be enthroned and we shall be about his feet with delight and devotion.

Blessed to be finally home.

Our hearts languish no more.

Martin Luther would say, "More light, Lord, more light."[149]

Now we are in the Presence of More Light, the Bright and Morning Star.[150]

LIGHT ETERNAL.

And He was there every second of our journey, guiding the righteous.

What a shining path it was and we weren't aware of the glow of God's Glory.

"For God who said, let light shine out of darkness – made His Light shine in our hearts to give us the light of the knowledge of the face of Christ."[151]

A godly saint by the name of Mrs. Campbell, in the book, *Stepping Heavenward*, pictures for us the fulfillment of a life lived out in the Light of her King in loving reverie.

She has lost all but Him.

With deep joy and release she looks toward HEAVEN.

When I read her testimony, tears spilled over my cheeks, because within me welled up a deep sensitive ache that I did not know that I had, a hunger for some place I've never been, joy unspeakable. It could only be described as being homesick. The old hymn *Beulah Land* came to mind.

The chorus says, "Beulah Land, I'm longing for you."

And I was.

I was longing for HEAVEN.

These are her words:

"It is only a question of days and my tired feelings will be over. Then I shall be as young and fresh as ever and shall have strength to praise and love God as I cannot do now. But before I go, I want once more to tell you how good He is, how blessed it is to suffer with Him, how infinitely happy He has made me in the very hottest heat of the furnace. It will strengthen your trials to recall my dying testimony. There is no wilderness so dreary that His love cannot illuminate it, no desolation so desolate but that He can sweeten it.

I know what I am saying.

It is no delusion.

I believe the highest, purest happiness is known only to those who have learned Christ in sickrooms, in poverty, in racking suspense and anxiety amid hardships and at the open grave.

To Learn Christ – this is life."[152]

She learned HIM and so must we.

Billy Bray, a Cornish miner, converted to Christ and turned minister in 1823, shouted as his dying word, "Glory!"[153]

Heaven was real to him.

The great American evangelist, D. L. Moody, spoke these final words as his heart gave way during his last evangelistic campaign.

"This is my triumph; this is my coronation day! I have been looking forward to it for years!"[154]

He was anticipating HEAVEN.

"This is the end,

    but for me

  It is the beginning

    Of life."[155]

        Dietrich Bonhoeffer

HEAVEN is a bright beginning.... Life lived in the Light of Jesus' Presence Forever.

What a path.

    Saved

    Sustained

    Satisfied

What a Light.

    Guiding

    Shining

    Reflecting His Love

What a Day.

    No more night

    Filled with Light

    Home in sight.

What a Savior.

Our Daystar.

The Bright and Morning Light.

Are you on the path of the righteous, dear reader?

The Daystar waits for you. Take a step toward Heaven.

"Our fair morning is at hand; the Daystar is near the rising, and we are not many miles from home. What matter, then of ill entertainment in the smoky inns of this worthless world? We are not here to stay, and we shall be dearly welcome to Him to whom we are going."[156]

Samuel Rutherford

DAYSTAR, SHINE DOWN ON ME.

Heaven awaits.

JOURNAL

What is your concept of Heaven?

Do you ever think about Heaven?

Are you bringing anyone along with you?

PRAYER

Father:

I need to be reminded of Heaven every day. It is my destiny. Hallelujah, I have one! Show me each day this shining Truth as I look into the faces of others who are caught up with earth's cares. Give me the desire to share YOUR LOVE with all I encounter along my path, sojourners just like me.

Same struggles,

Same Savior,

We all need Jesus.

Oh Lord, I will.

I want to bring YOUR Light to them.

Forgive me when I fail.

Keep me on the path.

Reveal YOUR Love to me;

Remind me of the promises to the righteous.

SHINE DOWN ON ME, BEAUTIFUL DAYSTAR.

Heaven awaits.

PROMISES FOR THE PATH

1. "The Lord does not let the *righteous* go hungry."
   Proverbs 10 3a

2. "Blessings crown the head of the *righteous*."
   Proverbs 10:6a

3. " The memory of the *righteous* will be a blessing."
   Proverbs 10:7a

4. "The mouth of the *righteous* is a fountain of life."
   Proverbs 10:11a

5. "The wages of the *righteous* bring them life."
   Proverbs 10:16a

6. "The tongue of the *righteous* is choice silver."
   Proverbs 10:20a

7. "The lips of the **righteous** nourish many."
   Proverbs 10:21a

8. "What the **righteous** desire will be granted."
   Proverbs 10:25b

9. "The prospect of the **righteous** is joy."
   Proverbs 10:28a

10. "The way of the Lord is a refuge for the
    righteous."
    Proverbs 10:29a

11. "The **righteous** will never be uprooted."
    Proverbs 10:30a

12. "The mouth of the **righteous** brings forth wisdom."
    Proverbs 10:32:a

13. " The **righteous** man is delivered from trouble."
    Proverbs 11:8a

14. "The truly **righteous** man obtains life."
    Proverbs 11:19a

15. "The **righteous** will thrive like a green leaf."
    Proverbs 11:28b

16. "The fruit of the **righteous** is a tree of life."
    Proverbs 11:30a

17. "The plans of the **righteous** are just."
Proverbs 12:5a

18. "The house of the **righteous** stands firm."
Proverbs 12:7b

19. "A **righteous** man cares for the needs of his animal."
Proverbs 12:10a

20. "The root of the **righteous** flourishes."
Proverbs 12:12b

21. "A **righteous** man is cautious in friendship."
Proverbs 12:26a

22. "The **righteous** hate what is false."
Proverbs 13:5a

23. "The light of the **righteous** shines brightly."
Proverbs 13:9a

24. "Prosperity is the reward of the **righteous**."
Proverbs 13:22b

25. "The house of the **righteous** contains great treasure."
Proverbs 15:6a

26. "The heart of the **righteous** weighs in answers."
Proverbs 15:28a

27. "When the **righteous** triumph, there is great elation."
Proverbs 28:12a

28. "When the **righteous** thrive, the people rejoice."
Proverbs 29:2a

29. "A **righteous** one can sing and be glad."
Proverbs 6b

30. "The **righteous** detest the dishonest."
Proverbs 29:27a

31. "The Lord hears the prayers of the **righteous**."
Proverbs 15:29b

These are promises for every day of the month.

God's Guiding Light continually breaks through, bringing His Truth to our lives.

I would love to hear from you.

How to Contact the Author

www.billiecash.com or *brcash@midsouth.rr.com*

Billie Cash
1605 N Germantown Pkwy; Suite 111
Cordova, TN 38018

NOTES

CHAPTER ONE: COMING INTO HIS LIGHT
The Upanishads: Brihadaranyaka Upanishad, 1.3.28

1. Krause: Richard Krause, *An English Forest*, (London: Constable and Company Limited, 1982) Back Cover

2. John 8:12

3. Ephesians 2:1

4. John 14:6

5. Phillips: John Phillips, *Only One Life*, (Neptune: Loizeau, 1995), 32

6. Ibid., 33

7. Keller: Helen Keller, *The Story Of My Life*, (Airmont Classic: Airmont), 19

8. II Samuel 22:29

9. Romans 8:16

CHAPTER TWO: THE LIGHT OF HIS FELLOWSHIP
Michelangelo: Buonarroti Michelangelo, Sonnet

10. *Martindale, Root*: Wayne Martindale and Jerry Root, *The Quotable Lewis, An Experiment in Criticism, Epilogue*, (Wheaton: Tyndale House, 1989), 140-141

11. Ibid., 137-138

12. *Millay*: Edna St. Vincent Millay, *Renascence* (1912), l. 1

13. Psalm 14:5

CHAPTER THREE: THE LIGHT OF HIS APPRAISAL
Lucretius: Titus Lucretius Carus, De Rerun, bk. 1 11176

14. Psalm 11:5a

15. *Maxwell:* John Maxwell, *Failing Forward* (Nashville: Thomas Nelson, 2000), 21

16. Ibid., 16

17. *Anderson,* Saucy: Neil Anderson and Robert Saucy, *The Common Made Holy* (Eugene: Harvest House 1997), 15

18. Ephesians 2:10

19. Jeremiah 18:6

20. Isaiah 45:9 NASB

21. Romans 9:21 NASB

22. *Gurnall:* William Gurnall, *The Christian in Complete Armour, Vol. I* (Edinburgh: The Banner of Truth Trust, 1995), 47

CHAPTER FOUR: THE LIGHT OF HIS SECURITY
Tillich: Paul Johannes Tillich, The Shaking of the Foundations, chapter 19

23. Hebrews 6:19

24. *Bonhoeffer:* Dietrich Bonhoeffer, Quoted in Bob and Michael Benson, *Disciplines For The Inner Life* (Waco: Word 1985), 94

25. Psalm 7:9b

26. John 17:11b

27. Acts 17:28

28. Deuteronomy 11:8

29. Psalm 37:25

30. I John 5:13

31. Ecclesiastes 12:1

32. *Addison:* Joseph Addison, *Horace, Odes,* bk. III, ode iii

33. *Selden:* John Selden, *Table Talk (1689). Bible, Scripture*

34. Psalm 91:1

35. Psalm 119:105

36. Romans 1:17

37. *Booth*: Edwin P. Booth, *Martin Luther*, (Uhrichsville: Barbour MCMXCV), 68

38. Hebrews 13:8

39. Proverbs 9:25b

CHAPTER FIVE: THE LIGHT OF HIS FAVOR
Newman, John Henry Cardinal Newman, Pindar, Pythian Odes VIII, 1, 135

40. *Virgil*: (Publius Vergilius Maro) *Georgics*, I, 1.40

41. *Kierkegaard*: Soren Kierkegaard, *The Prayers of Kierkegaard*, Perry Lebre, ed. (Chicago: University of Chicago, 1956), 147

42. Psalm 5:12

43. *Hammarskjold*: Dag Hammarskjold: Quoted in Bob and Michael Benson, *Disciplines For The Inner Life* (Waco: Word 1985), 281

44. *Richardson*: Michael Richardson, *Amazing Faith*, (Colorado Springs:WaterBrook Press, 2000), 21

45. Ibid., 22

46. *Chesterton*: G. K. Chesterton, *Orthodoxy,* Foreword, (Colorado Springs: WaterBrook Press, 1994), xvii

47. Ibid., ix

CHAPTER SIX: THE LIGHT OF HIS DELIVERANCE
Thomas: Dylan Thomas, Light Breaks Where No Sun Shines, l, 1

48. *Chatham*: Judith McCart Chatham, *A Whirlwind's Breath* (Carmel: Guild Press 1998), 84

49. *Addison*: Joseph Addison, *Ode* (in The Spectator, no. 465, August 23, 1712), 2

50. Psalm 8:2

51. II Chronicles 20:21-22

52. Psalm 32:7b

53. *Day:* Albert Edward Day, *An Autobiography of Prayer* (New York: Harper and Brothers 1952), 45

54. Job 35:10

55. *Sankey*: Ira Sankey, *Sacred Songs and Solos* (Edinburgh, London: Marshall, Morgan and Scott Ltd), 459

56. Proverbs 3:5-6

57. Ephesians 5:8, 9, 14

58. *Cash, Chatham,* Billie Cash and Judy Chatham, *Windows of Assurance*, (Greenville, Belfast: Ambassador Emerald International 2001), 136

59. *Gariepy*: Henry Gariepy, *Songs in the Night*, (Grand Rapids: William B. Erdmans 1996), 137

CHAPTER SEVEN; A SHINING PASSION
Goethe: Johann Wolfgang Von Goethe, Elective Affinities, pt. 11, ch. 3

60. Curtis, Eldredge: Brent Curtis and John Eldredge, *The Sacred Romance* (Nashville: Thomas Nelson 1997), 19

61. Isaiah 58:12b

62. Psalm 42:1-2

63. Beumer: Jurjen Beumer, *Henri Nowen A Restless Seeking for God* (New York: Crossroad 1997), 33

64. Ibid., 22

65. *Augustine*: Augustine, *The Confessions,* Philip Burton ed. (London: Everyman 2001), I, 7

66. Ibid., III, 1

67. *Petersen,Hutchinson*: William Petersen and Warner A. Hutchinson, *The Autobiography of Madame Guyon* (New Canaan: Keats 1980), 43

68. *Curtis, Eldredge:* Brent Cutis and John Eldredge Quoted in *The Sacred Romance Epilogue (Nashville:Thomas Nelson 1997), 195*

CHAPTER EIGHT; A SHINING PRAYING
Milton: John Milton, Paradise Lost, 111,1.1

69. Lamentations 3:22-24

70. Isaiah 62:6a

71 Lamentations 2:19a

72. Isaiah 59:15b-16a

73. Hebrews 7:24-25

74. Ezra 10:11a

75. Ephesians 5:18

76. Ephesians 6:10-18

77. *Foster*: Richard Foster, *Prayer* (San Francisco: Harper 1992), 2

78. *Nowen*: Henri Nowen, *Here and Now* (New York: Crossroad 2000), 88

79. *Carmichael*: Amy Carmichael, *Gold Cord* (Fort Washington: Christian Literature Crusade 1957), 22

80. Ibid., 284

81. Ibid., 210

CHAPTER NINE: A SHINING PEACE
Newman: John Henry Cardinal Newman, The Pillars of Cloud, Lead Kindly Light, st.1

82. *L'Engle*: Madeleine L'Engle, *Walking On Water*: Reflections on Faith and Art (New York: North Point Press 1980), 11

83. *Chambers*: Oswold Chambers, *Studies in Sermon On The Mount* (Totnes: Oswold Chambers Publications Association 1995), 13

84. *Wilkerson*: Bruce Wilkerson, *Secrets of The Vine* (Sisters; Multonomah 2001), 86

85. *McCasland*: David McCasland, *Abandoned To God*, (Nashville: Thomas Nelson 1993), 131

86. Isaiah 26:3

87. *Kelly*: Thomas R. Kelly, *A Testament Of Devotion* (San Francisco: Harper 1992), 9

88. Ibid., 15

89. *Laurent*: Bob Laurent, *Watchman Nee* (Uhrichsville: Barbour MCMXCVIII), 9

90. Ibid., 9

91. Ibid., 10

CHAPTER TEN; CONTINUING EVER BRIGHTER
Tennyson: Alfred Lord Tennyson, In Memoriam, 50, st. 1

92. II Corinthians 4:16

93. I Chronicles 16:12a

94. John 15:4

95. Hebrews 13:5b-6

96. *Curry, Mercer*: Dayna Curry and Heather Mercer, *Prisoners Of Hope* (New York: Doubleday 2002), 234-235

97. *Elliot*: Elisabeth Elliot, *Through Gates of Splendor*, Epilogue II (Crossings Classic: 1981), 258

98. Ibid., 165-166

99. *Eaton*: Betty Sue Eaton, *Listening to the Garden Grow* (Walpole: Stillpoint 1996), 41

100. *Elliot*: Elisabeth Elliot, *Through Gates of Splendor,* Epilogue II (Crossings Classic: 1981), 263

CHAPTER ELEVEN; SUSTAINED EVER BRIGHTER
Wharton: Edith Wharton, Vesaliusin Zante

101. *Keats*: John Keats, *Ode To A Grecian Urn*, st. 3

102. Psalm 19:8

103. *Wordsworth*: William Wordsworth, *Lines Composed a Few Miles Above Tintern Abbey* (1798) XIV, I. 444

104. Psalm 119:130

105. *Browning*: Robert Browning, *Saul* (1855), st. 18

106. I Thessalonians 1:3

CHAPTER TWELVE; RENEWED EVER BRIGHTER
Shakespeare: William Shakespeare, Othello V, ii, 7

107. Psalm 27:51

108. *Bradley*: James Bradley, *Flags of Our Fathers* (New York: Bantam 2000), 12

109. Ibid., 19

110. I Kings 15:1-3

111. *Emerson*: Ralph Waldo Emerson, *The Conduct of Life* (1860), Fate

112. *Shakespeare*: William Shakespeare, *Hamlet,* III, iii, 150

113. Philippians 3:13-14

114. Isaiah 43:19-20

115. Jeremiah 15:19

CHAPTER THIRTEEN; FOLLOWING HIS LIGHT HOME
Shelley: Percy Bysshe Shelley, Adonais, st. 52

116. *Martindale, Root*: Wayne Martindale and Jerry Root, *The Quotable Lewis* (Wheaton: Tyndale 1989), 287

117. Ecclesiastes 3:11

118. *Buchanan:* Mark Buchanan, *Things Unseen* (Sisters: Multnomah 2002),157

119. I Peter 2:16-17; The Message

120. Philippians 4:8a

121. Genesis 15:1b

122. Revelation 22:5

123. Revelation 21:23

124. Revelation 21:21

125. Revelation 21:19-20; 21:12-21

126. *Curtis, Eldredge*: Brent Curtis and John Eldredge, *The Sacred Romance* (Nashville: Thomas Nelson 1997), 201

127. *Bayley*: Joseph Bayley, *Heaven* (Elgin: David C. Cook 1987), 21-23

128. Revelation 5:8

129. Revelation 21:26

130. Revelation 19:5-6

131. Revelation 22:3-4

132. *Lutzer*: Erwin W. Lutzer, *One Minute After You Die* (Chicago: Moody 1997), 89

133. Revelation 21:4

134. Revelation 7:17; 21:4

135. Revelation 21:4

136. Revelation 21:27

137. Revelation 7:6

138. Psalm 14:5

139. Psalm 11:5

140. Psalm 7:9

141. Psalm 5:12

142. Psalm 30:7b

143. Philippians 12:14b

144. *Yancy*: Philip Yancy, *Reaching For The Invisible God*, (Grand Rapids: Zondervan 2000), 72

145. Revelation 19:9

146. Revelation 19:6-9

147. Revelation 19:1-4

148. Revelation 4:10

149. *Booth*: Edwin P. Booth, *Martin Luther*, (Uhrichsville: Barbour MCMXCV), 311

150. Revelation 12:16b

151. II Corinthians 4:6

152. *Prentiss*: Elizabeth Prentiss, *Stepping Heavenward* (Uhrichsville: Barbour MCMXCVIII), 312

153. *Lawson*: James Gilchrist Lawson, *Deeper Experiences of Famous Christians* (Uhrichsville: Barbour MCMXCIX), 230

154. Ibid., 294

155. *Arnold*: Duane W. H. Arnold, *Prayers of Martyrs* (Grand Rapids: Zondervan: 1991), 102

156. *Lytle*: Clyde Francis Lytle, *Leaves of Gold, Anthology* (Fort Worth: Brownlow 1948), 41

ENDOMENTS

"Our journey through life is more abundant when we focus on who we are in Christ and what we are here for. Take some time with Billie's new book "Light Breaking Through" which is beautifully written and God inspired. You will find encouragement and guidance for your life choices as you draw closer and allow HIM to be the light in your life."

Donna Brindel
Women's Ministry Director, Virginia Beach VA

"Here I was -- a 46 year old wife, mother of a five year old, a corporate executive of a fortune 500 company desperately needing my Sunday afternoon to "catch up," when I opened your wonderful book entitled "Light Breaking Through", Trusting God's Timing. I was unable to put it down.   I saw a little piece of myself in each illustration. Billie, you have taught me that my blessing could be rich in the Lord if I would slow down, stop and seek the Lord's guidance in all things.   Life would be easier to live.   I can be prepared for the best and the worst that may come my way. I have felt the presence of the Lord today and my Sunday has been filled with a peace. I can be a better wife, mother, employee, friend -- woman. Thank you for sharing this life changing, thought provoking, masterfully written book with me."

Sheila Harrell
Vice president Customer Service Federal Express Corporation

" Wonderful. Your style is powerful.   This should be a blessing to many."

D. J. Borchers, Captain, US Navy(Retired)

"Light Breaking Through" is a walk with a wise, trusted friend.   Billie's unassuming self disclosure provides a glimpse into many facets of her life -- a life where any woman can find pieces of herself.   Whether she is relating as a girl unsure of herself, a performer preparing for the stage, a student finding God in poetry, a young mother experiencing daily challenges, a loving wife preparing for her husband's homecoming, or a grandmother sharing her life with her family and all God's children, Billie's love for God and life is evident and contagious.   Using her own life experiences, as well as wisdom from an elaborate array of great writers and philosophers, Billie beautifully illustrates the rewards, both gentle and grand, of trusting God's light to lead us to His perfect will.   "Light Breaking Through" feels like a very personal gift.   Billie has taken my world -- a world of books, academia, and Christian womanhood -- and held it up to the Light.   The light that illuminates, cleanses, heals, and nourishes."

Susan DeCarlo
Writing and Literature Instructor, University of Memphis
PhD candidate